resident mockery

give us an hour for magic

We of the purple glove

We of the starling flight

    & velvet hour

We of arabic pleasure's breed

We of sundome & the night

from   AN AMERICAN PRAYER
by
James Douglas Morrison

JIM *MORRISON*

AN HOUR FOR MAGIC

**PHOTOGRAPHS, TEXT
and DESIGN by
FRANK LISCIANDRO**

PLEXUS, LONDON

For Rose Lisciandro, with love.

Copyright © 1982, 1993 by Frank Lisciandro
Published by Plexus Publishing Limited
26 Dafforne Road, London SW17 8TZ
First printing 1993

This book could not have been completed
without the help of the following people.
I sincerely thank all of you: Kathie Hayes,
Tom Matthews, John & Janet Lengsfelder,
Corky Courson, Bob Gover, The Garetti Family,
John Clark, Richard Linnell, Bill Siddons,
The Doors & Jack Kerouac.

Black and white photographs printed by Tom Ploch
(Barrie Schwortz Studios)

British Library in Publication Data

Lisciandro, Frank
    Jim Morrison – An Hour For Magic
    Photojournal. – 2Rev.ed
    I. Title
    782.42166092

ISBN 0 85965 162 2

First published in England by Eel Pie Publishing

Printed in Great Britain by Bath Press Colourbooks
Cover design by Keith Pointing

CONTENTS

AN INTRODUCTION

Twenty two years ago a friend died in Paris, France. For several years I could not accept the fact that I would neither see nor talk with him again. In my dreams we met on highways and in bars, and his appearance was as I had last seen him. During those years I found it painful to speak about him, or read his poems or listen to his songs.

Fortunately, time is the greatest healer and the most patient. Today, I can once again enjoy the subtle irony of Jim Morrison's poetry and the expressive power of his recorded voice. His creations vitalize, inspire, and enrich me with their intriguingly inventive observations and entertainments.

★ ★ ★ ★ ★ ★ ★ ★ ★ ★ ★ ★ ★ ★ ★ ★ ★ ★

In 1968 I quit a good paying, responsible position with a prestigious educational/documentary film company to accept the challenge of editing *Feast of Friends*, a documentary film being made about The Doors. Although Jim and I were at the UCLA Film School in 1964 and 1965, it was not until I started working on *Feast* that we really got to know each other.

Paul Ferrara, the cameraman, had captured the transcendent magic of the Doors' live performances and Jim's wild stage presence. Ten hours of powerful images shot at concerts and recording studios, in limos, planes, monorails and backstage dressing rooms had been recorded, processed and workprinted. It was raw, emotional and evocative footage, but it was not a movie. There was no script or plan of how the scenes would be assembled, nor was there a unifying point of view or theme. Paul and the members of the band assumed that I would bring organization to the project, and in the process help construct a finished film out of the unconnected visuals. For the first few weeks, as I reviewed and logged the scenes, everyone dropped in to offer me advice and suggestions. Watching someone else edit film can be as boring as watching rocks grow and before long I was all alone with the visuals.

My editing space, a small room at the back of the lower floor of the Doors office, was hot, cramped and cluttered with sound gear, yet it could not be better located. If the film was about Jim and the Doors and how their music reflected and commented on the 60's, then I was fitting the pieces together right in the eye of the L.A. rock hurricane.

My usual schedule was to start work mid-afternoon and stay late, constructing the scenes and re-cutting them until I felt they would play. One evening as I sat alone in front of the moviola screen watching a sequence of the Doors at the Singer Bowl in New York City, I felt a presence in the room, as if a cool breeze had entered and swirled around me. My skin tingled and the hair on the back of my head stood up at frozen attention. I turned quickly, ready to fight or flee depending on the size of the presence.

Jim stood a few feet behind me intently watching the screen over my shoulder.

"Don't want to bother you," he said smiling.

"No man, I didn't hear you come in," I said, trying not to sound jumpy. "Why don't you grab that chair and I'll run this back from the beginning."

As I re-wound the film, Jim moved a chair up to the small screen and handed me a bottle of Superior beer. Even unedited and without live sound, the concert footage had the edgy tension of an impending explosion.

At one point, the screen showed Jim lying on the stage, writhing snakelike and singing, while a dozen or more burly New York cops stood in a semi-circle around him. The police actually prowled the stage and acted as barriers against the fans who tried repeatedly to get to one of the Doors. Jim continued singing and gyrating while the band pumped out the music and the fans kept coming at the cops, rushing the stage with a fatal persistence. The jarring immediacy of the wide angle lens, floating hand-held camera and green tint of the neon lighting gave the scene an unbalanced, bizarre quality.

"Do you intentionally provoke those kids?" I asked.

"I try to give them a good time. They rush the stage because the cops are there and that's a challenge they can't resist."

"It looks like they want to get to you, to touch you, or yank out some hair as a souvenir."

"Maybe some of them want to, but mostly they're just letting off steam and reacting to the cops."

"I don't get it."

"It's like a game. The kids try to get passed the cops and the cops try to stop them. There are no rules at a rock concert. Anything is possible."

"Let's look at it again," he said, getting up to get us each another beer. "Maybe we can use "Not To Touch The Earth" as the soundtrack."

For the next two hours we worked with the footage, shifting shots, adding music, cutting weak moments, until the scene played seamlessly.

"I should probably get back to the recording studio," Jim said as I locked up the editing room. "See what the cats are doing."

"Thanks for the help," I said.

"If you want to see how audiences react at our concerts you should come with us next week. We're doing gigs in Virginia, Atlantic City and ... somewhere else ... Saratoga, I think."

"Sounds great."

"Maybe you can take some pictures," Jim suggested.

He strolled off towards the Elektra recording studio with a slow, slouch-shouldered amble. He did not seem to have a worry and he surely was not in any hurry. He was the essence of relaxed.

I photographed Jim and the band both on and off the stage during that three city, East Coast tour. He and I gradually became close friends, traveling, working and hanging out together. Over the next three years, I watched him change from a slinky rock idol to a great bearded poet; the physical transformation marked an alteration in the road he traveled.

Jim Morrison was a complex man of enormous talent who seemed to live by William Blake's proverb: "The road of excess leads to the palace of wisdom."

Despite his sometimes exaggerated excess, I found Jim to be intelligent, sensitive, funny, and generous. The following pages reveal the man I knew. He is not at all the same person others, who did not know him nearly as well, have described. If you look closely into the highlights and shadows of my photographs, and listen to the nuances that resonate from his words, you might discover someone you'll never forget.

These are the first words I've written about Jim for publication and only a small number of my photos have ever been seen before. The photos are in a loose chronological order. Near the middle of the book Jim's physical appearance begins to change. He evolved into his self-image of a poet.

Many of Jim's poems that appear in these pages are published with the kind permission of Corky Courson.

Robert Gover, author of seven novels, including the '60's bestseller *One Hundred Dollar Misunderstanding,* has contributed a reminiscence of Jim in 1967. They were close friends, and Jim would have liked to have played a part in bringing Bob's novel, *The Maniac Responsible,* to the movie Screen.

Some of Jim's other friends appear in the book:

Kathy Lisciandro worked, for a time, as Jim's and the Doors' secretary. She helped Jim edit his book *An American Prayer* and typed his poems and correspondence.

Babe Hill worked on both of Jim's films, *Feast of Friends* and *HWY*, and was, during the last two years of Jim's life, his closest and most trusted friend.

Paul Ferrara did the cinematography for Jim's films and still photography for the Doors.

Bill Siddons was the Doors' personal manager for almost their entire career, but his admiration and respect for Jim transcended business.

Pamela Courson Morrison was Jim's soulmate, refuge and friend. He dedicated his books to her and left her everything when he died.

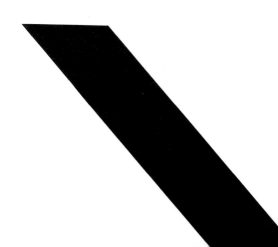

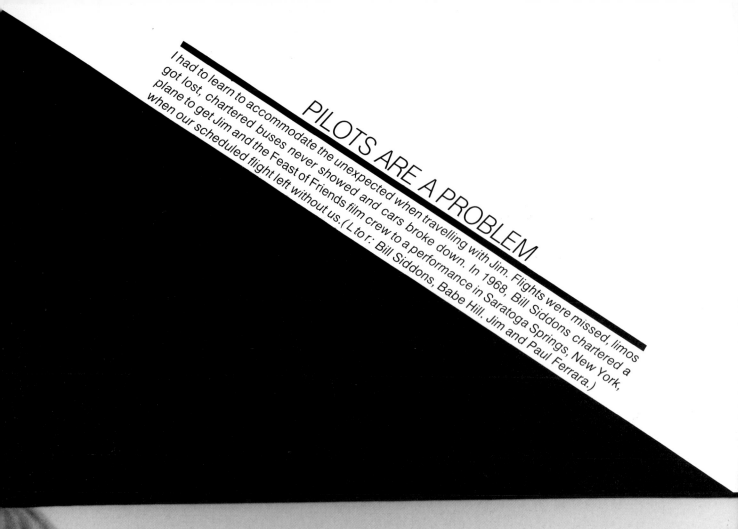

PILOTS ARE A PROBLEM

I had to learn to accommodate the unexpected when travelling with Jim. Flights were missed, limos got lost, chartered buses never showed and cars broke down. In 1968, Bill Siddons chartered a plane to get Jim and the Feast of Friends film crew to a performance in Saratoga Springs, New York, when our scheduled flight left without us. (L to r: Bill Siddons, Babe Hill, Jim and Paul Ferrara.)

Of the great insane American Night we sing
Sending our gift to its vast promise.

Pilots are a problem
The rain and hungry sea
greedy for steel
Say a soft American Prayer
A quiet animal sigh
for the strong plane landing

We rode on opium tires
from the colossal airport chess game
at dawn
New from glass
& broken night
Landed then in quiet fog
beside the times
out of this strange river

Then gladly through a wasted morning
Happy to be alive to signs of life
                    a dog
                    a school girl
Are we in Harlem?

                              (JDM)

*We appeal to the same human needs
as classical tragedy and early Southern
blues. Think of it as a seance in an
environment which has become hostile to
life; cold, restrictive. People feel
they're dying in a bad landscape. So
they gather together in a seance in order
to invoke, palliate, and drive away the
dead through chanting, singing, dancing
and music. They try to cure an illness,
to bring back harmony into the world.*

(JDM)

At precisely the time ordered, the sleek, fat, black limos pulled up to the front of the Warwick Hotel in Manhattan to transport us to the gig.

Ray, Robbie and the Doors' manager, Bill Siddons, dashed out of the lobby and into the lead limo, even before it had rolled to a complete stop. Bill had a million last minute knotty details to unravel, so their limo sped off to the auditorium, leaving Babe Hill, John Densmore, Paul Ferrara and I waiting for Jim. He was not usually late for concerts but he had the upsetting practice of arriving backstage only minutes before he was supposed to go on.

"Did you call his room?" John asked no one in particular.

"I called. He ain't there." Paul was resigned to wait.

"I'll go look in the bar," I volunteered, hoping to have time for a quick beer.

"Don't get lost, man."

"I'll go with you," said Babe.

Jim wasn't in the bar, or in the restaurant, and another call to his room proved equally futile.

John was pacing, anxious about arriving on time.

"He'll show up," said Paul. "You guys kill me. After all this time you know how he is."

"Maybe he's asleep and doesn't hear the phone," John guessed. "Think I'll go up and pound on his door. What room is he in?"

"1208," said Babe, "but I'm sure he ain't there."

As John set out toward the elevators, I spotted Jim coming into the lobby from the hotel's side entrance, a knock-out brunette holding his arm. They were in deep, private conversation. Jim noticed us across the lobby, stopped and gave the woman a tender farewell kiss. She held onto him, staring into his face. He said something to her, she nodded, kissed him quickly and rushed away.

As Jim approached us, I remembered John and ran to stop him just as he was about to enter an "Up" elevator.

"John, he's here!"

"Oh. . . . ." John jumped out of the elevator an instant before the doors closed. "Where was he?"

I never saw the brunette again, and wonder if Jim did. He never even mentioned her name, being very discreet about the women he knew. I can't recall hearing him talk about any of his lady friends in macho terms. He was a genuine Southern gentleman and believed that gallantry, charm and a dash of manners were the ingredients to win a woman's heart.

We got into the limo and started out for the city in Connecticut where the concert was being held. Jim was in a reflective mood, staring out the window at the carnival of colored lights, cars and people on the streets.

As we drove out of midtown, he joined our conversation about the Howling Wolf show we had seen the night before. As usual, he was soft spoken and thoughtfully articulate, as if he wanted us to know what he really meant and how he felt. Since he made every word count, I always understood and usually remembered what he said, although I often disagreed with him. In casual conversations his voice would get so faint I had to strain to hear him. He listened with the same thoughtful attention to what other people had to say. It was only on stage, or when he had too much to drink, that his voice became loud, vibrant, gruff, deep, quick and mindless.

The limo ride was pleasant and before long we were off the highway and on suburban streets of tastefully painted houses fronted by clipped hedges, flat lawns and paving stone walkways. It didn't look right.

I leaned over the front seat and asked the driver, "Where are we?"

"Ah . . . I just got off the Merritt Parkway and now I'm supposed to look for. . . ." He consulted a sheet of typed directions attached to a clipboard.

"You know, I ain't ever really been up here before," he admitted.

We were lost! Lost in a limo somewhere in Connecticut. It was already past 9:30 p.m. and the Doors were scheduled to appear on stage at 10 o'clock. If we didn't find our way we'd almost surely be late. The promoters would be pissed off and the audience would be restless and unruly and not easy to please.

The rest of the ride was like a comedy script, but all the laughs were born of frustration and tension. It went something like this:

LOST IN THE LIMO

Frank: "So do you know where we are, or what?"
Driver: "Well, according to this we were supposed to get off at Park Avenue and . . . ."
John: "What's the matter?"
Frank: "We appear to be lost at the moment."
Babe: "What?!"
Jim: "Why does this always happen to me?"
Paul: "Who's that in back of us?"
John: "Looks like the other limo."
Babe: "It can't be, unless they're lost too."
Driver: "No, it's not them."
Paul: "However, they do seem to know us. They're stopping."
Jim: "Well let's ask them for directions."

Our limo stops and the car travelling behind pulls up. It's a teenage couple playing let's-see-who-is-in-the-limo. Jim slinks down in the seat, hiding his face.

Driver: "Hey, we need some directions."
Teenage guy: "Where do you want to go?"
Driver: "To the Municipal Auditorium."
Teenage girl: "You want to go the other way. You took the wrong turn on Park Avenue."
Teenage boy: "Just go up here and turn around."

Driver: "Thanks."
Teenage boy: "Hey! Who are you guys?"
Babe: "The Mamas and the Papas."

Even Jim has to laugh as we drive away.

Driver: "I'll try to turn around."
Jim: "We are deep in the heart of nowhere."
John: "Look out! That car is going to broadside us! . . ."

The driver takes surprisingly quick evasive action. Everyone sighs with relief. The driver continues trying to U-turn the monster car in the narrow street.

Paul: "Stop! . . . there's a ravine back here, partner."
Babe: "Oh, the ineptitude!"
Jim: "Let's find a store or gas station and ask someone where we are."
Babe: "Why don't you turn on your high beams?"
Driver: "I got 'em on."

The residential streets have gradually given way to an industrial area and miles of warehouses.

9:50 P.M.

John: "There are no street signs anywhere."
Jim: "Deeper and deeper into the interior, wilderness calls. . . ."
Babe: "This is no time for poems, Jim."
Paul: "This'll only be the third gig you guys have been late for . . . this month."
Jim: "How can you be late to your own funeral?"

A bright street looms ahead. A sign clearly indicates that it is Park Avenue. The limo pauses at the intersection. The driver looks one way and then the other.

John: "Now what do we do?"
Someone: "Right."
Someone else: "Left"
Babe: "You don't want to turn left, man. That's the way we just came from."
Driver: "According to the directions, it says left."
Babe: "Let me see that."

Babe reads the directions. Looks out the window.

Babe: "These directions are all wrong. Fire the guy who wrote them."

Despite Babe's unshakeable conviction, the driver makes a left and we are at last on a brightly lit street.

10:00 P.M.

John: "I don't think we're on the right street."
Driver: "We're on Park Avenue."
John: "Yeah, well, I think it just changed."
Driver: "You think so?"
John: "Yeah, when you get to the next intersection slow down. . . ."
Paul: "We're only going five miles an hour now, John."
Driver: "That looks like a major street up there."
John: "Let's check the street sign."
Three voices: "No street sign."
Driver: "These little towns are noted for that."
Paul: "Look, a sidewalk. We're saved!"

We have left the industrial area and are once again in a residential part of the city.

10:10 P.M.

Jim: "Let's go knock on one of these doors and ask somebody."

Babe simulates knocking on a door.

Babe: "Ah, excuse me ma'am, we're all rock 'n' roll stars and we're trying to find our way to the concert. . . ."
Frank: "We're coming to a dead end."
Jim: "Typical, typical, typical."
Paul: "I think we should find a phone and call somebody."
John: "Who?"
Paul: "At this point, anybody will do."
Jim: "Let's ask that guy."
Driver: "What guy?"
Jim: "That guy. Oh, too late. He saw us and ran for cover."
Babe: "Let's go back to where we made the wrong turn. . . ."
Paul: "Who's got a cigarette?"
Babe: "I'm all out."

Paul: "Great."
Jim: "Typical, typical, typical."

10:20 P.M.

Frank: "Here's a guy pulling out."
Jim: "Ask him. Stop and ask him."

The driver pulls up to a middle-aged guy parked in a car. Jim turns down his window.

Jim: "Do you know how to get to the Auditorium?"
Guy: "What auditorium?"

Three voices: "The JFK Municipal Auditorium."

Guy: "You go back down and take a right and follow it till you see the Parkway and then you get on the Parkway headed for New York and I don't know where in New York it is.

We all groan.

Jim: "No, it's here, not in New York."

Guy: "Here? Then I don't know. . . ."
Jim: "Thanks.'

The limo pulls away.

Jim: "That's the last time I'll ever ask that bozo for directions."
Paul: "You just can't get any respect."
Babe: "OK, let's go back to where we made the turn I said not to make and go the way I said. OK?"

10:30 P.M.

Babe was right, the directions were wrong and we were fifty minutes late in arriving. Bill Siddons was pacing at the backstage entrance, but the audience was menacingly silent. Jim and John hurried to the dressing room. Within five minutes of our arrival The Doors were on their way to the stage.

★ ★ ★ ★ ★ ★ ★ ★ ★ ★ ★ ★ ★ ★ ★ ★ ★

"What shall we start with, 'Break on Through'?" Jim asked the other three Doors as they walked from the dressing room to the wings of the stage.
"Yeah."
"Why not?"
"O.K. with me, man."

The lights dimmed and the stage was veiled in absolute blackness. A roar lifted in the vast and overflowing auditorium. While the Doors assumed their places on the darkened stage, the sound swelled and expanded: a full range of voices screaming, yelling, whistling and shouting. This was accompanied by thunderous clapping and booming foot stomping. Did anyone hear the MC announce, "Hey, people, from Los Angeles, California . . . THE DOORS!"? The racket was so loud that Ray and Robbie could barely hear John's opening drum beats. It took all the intuition developed over countless hours of playing together for Ray to match his piano bass to John's drum rhythm. The audience was now louder than the band would be anytime during the concert. Robbie could feel Ray's big, fat bass notes and he slid his guitar into the song.

Jim waited, letting the band vamp until he knew the audience was at the very peak of its long pent-up hysteria. At the exact second the audience's howl could get no louder, Jim screamed with the full volume of 24,000 watts of amplification. He screamed as only a person who knows how to let the scream fly free—without restrictions, without fear of damaged vocal cords—can scream. It sounded like a thousand dogs whining at a thousand untuned violins mixed with the air-ripping roar of a squad of jet fighter planes. The sound screamed him.

Not one person in the audience had ever imagined, much less heard, such a sound. It shocked them into almost complete silence. At that moment the stage lights finally came on. The kids could now both see and hear the band playing.

Into that exact crack of illuminated and hypnotic attention, Jim sang the first words of the song:

You know the day destroys the night
Night divides the day
Tried to run
Tried to hide
Break on through to the other side
Break on through to the other side
Break on through, break on through
Break, break, break, break

It really didn't matter what words he sang because he had captured their spirits. Their attention and eyes would be focused on him for as long as he was on stage. Jim could do whatever he pleased: turn his back, dance, recite poems, play maracas, dive into the audience. He would not lose his control of them. They had already surrendered their impressionable, malleable minds, warm wet hearts, lovely liquid eyes, and slippery spirits to him, and he was going to take them on a trip, maybe as powerful as any they had ever experienced.

As the evening rocked from song to song, Jim caressed, cajoled, consoled, cursed, challenged and seduced. His power was a visible entity, like laser beams are visible energy. I imagined him holding a long lasso which encircled and bound the entire audience. If he slackened the rope's tension they would sway, fall apart and become restless. When he pulled on the lasso to rein them in tight, the whole audience would be on its collective toes staring and straining with rapturous tension. He had direct contact with each and every member of the audience.

Because Jim was so totally unpredictable, the kids had to pay close attention so as not to miss a vital movement or gesture. They watched his eyes to see where his trip was taking him. It could be chaos, terror, violence, death, nightmare, or it could be gentle rebirth and joy. He seemed at times blinded by a mystic light, lost and reeling. He teetered on the edge of the stage, ready perhaps to fall into those hungry eyes that devoured him. He swayed, staggered, lost his balance and regained it. It was scary and thrilling. The kids in the audience knew that Jim was not kidding them. This was no Mick Jagger dancing fool act, no good-time rock 'n' roll band, no gutsy girl singer, no peace and flowers trip. It wasn't exactly fun either. This was more like the severed reality of a vivid dream or an accident. You never knew what was going to happen next.

On stage that night, I saw Jim become a shaman, a wizard, a sorcerer, a magician, a medicine man, a witch doctor, an enchanter and a Dionysian reveler.

According to mythology, Dionysius wandered the world attended by a wine-frenzied troop of nymphs, satyrs, maenads and bacchantes. In most typical representations, Dionysius is shown as a youthful god, handsome, beardless, with long hair, sometimes riding a panther, other times wearing animal skins. Needless to say, women worshipped him with great fervor.

As a god he represented both the intoxicating and the beneficial aspects of wine. His worship resulted in riotous revelry and debauchery, but it also gave birth to culture. The festivals in his honor in Athens produced the earliest Greek theatrical performances.

That possessed, god-imitating reveler, who danced and shouted in such frenzied abandon, personified the power and mystery of the god and served to give fire and substance to the ancient myths.

Myths, fables and legends are the very foundation of society since they define man's role in the cosmic scenario. Myths give man meaning and purpose. All the original art forms: painting, sculpture, lyric and narrative poetry, architecture and theater were used as vehicles to depict and portray these primary stories.

In this exact same way, Jim and The Doors used the rock 'n' roll LP album and the concert stage as a theater of myths. The theater pieces were comprised of: 1) The Doors music creating the evocative mood; 2) the words of the songs retelling the legends; 3) Jim playing the ancient, possessed reveler, the actor who personified the god. The themes of the songs were the themes of the myths: birth, love, death, revenge, madness, murder, danger, transformation, primeval sensuality and homage to primal furies. Jim was the first rocker to reunite all of the elements of theater and restore them to original use. It was like street theater or a happening. It was guerilla theater, the Living Theater, and mime.

Sometimes I like to look at the history of Rock 'n' Roll like the origin of Greek drama, which started out on a threshing floor at the crucial seasons and was originally a band of worshippers, dancing and singing. Then, one day, a possessed person jumped out of the crowd and started imitating a god.   (JDM)

For the theater to work and for the myth to have more than just cognitive meaning, people had to feel it, internalize it. Rituals, seances and religious ceremonies provide opportunities for participants to experience mystic substance at gut level.

On stage, Jim underwent a complete metamorphosis: his soft gentle voice became raspy, husky, deep and powerful; his slouchy stance became arrogant, proud; his placid face turned into a thousand masks of tension and emotion; and his eyes, usually so penetrating and searching, turned vacant, glazed over and stared out at the audience like two bright windows. With this clairvoyant stare, Jim seemed to be looking into either the future or the past.

He made strange animal sounds, screamed and cried out as if in pain. His leather or snakeskin clothes crinkled and groaned as he moved. His movements and gestures became fitful and spasmodic, like a person in seizure. He danced, not with graceful and fluid motions, but with short hopping steps and piston like motions, bent forward, head snapping up and down. He moved like an American Indian performing a ritual dance.

On stage, Jim became the shaman. The shaman acquires his profession by inheriting the soul of a dead shaman. When the time is ripe, that soul responds to a call from the supernatural powers and the shaman begins to practice. No one can choose to be a shaman, nor can a person study for the job.

Shamans cure the sick, change the luck of the tribe, drive out evil spirits and go into ecstatic trances to foresee and foretell events distant in time and space. Those present at the ceremony are not mere objective spectators, but faithful believers. It is their belief that gives the shaman his power.

Shamans use songs, rhythms and dances in the ritual, which always take place at night, in an enclosed space.

For a long time, my logical, pragmatic mind kept asking: how can an American–born son of a Navy Admiral of Scottish-Irish heritage transform himself into a primitive sorcerer?

In the seance, the shaman led. A sensuous panic, deliberately evoked through drugs, chants, dancing, hurls the shaman into trance. Changed voice, convulsive movement. He acts like a madman. These professional hysterics, chosen precisely for their psychotic leaning, were once esteemed. They mediated between man and spirit-world. Their mental travels formed the crux of the religious life of the tribe.   (JDM)

Then one night, Jim, in complete lucid honesty, told Paul Ferrara, Babe Hill and I, a story that satisfied even my skepticism. It was the story of how, while travelling with his parents in a car, somewhere in the Southwest, they encountered a horrible accident and a fantastic event happened to Jim. The story was, fortunately, preserved on tape:

Ya know, the first time I discovered death—Me and my mother and father, and I'm not sure if my sister was there or whether she was alive or not, and my grandmother and grandfather, were driving through the desert at dawn . . . and a truckload of Indian workers had either hit another car or I don't know what happened, but there were Indians scattered all over the highway; bleeding to death. So, we, the car pulls up and stops. And it's my first reaction to death. I must have been about four or five. Up to then, man, my whole trip was . . . ah . . . that locks the car door when you push that thing, or you can look out the window and . . . ooh! I don't even remember if I'd seen a movie, man. And all of a sudden these are redskins, ya know, and they're just lying all over the road bleeding to death.

We came along after it happened. So they pulled the car up and they stop, and . . . uh . . . I'm just a kid so I have to stay in the car with my mother, ya know. And my father and my grandfather go back and check it out. And that was my first reaction to death, and I don''t know whether I'm crazy or what, but I had the feeling when that happened . . . like I didn't want to look back. I'm just this little . . . like a child is a flower, man, whose head is just floating in the breeze, man. But the reaction I get now

thinking back, looking back, is that possibly, the soul of one of those Indians, maybe several of them, just ran over and jumped into my brain.

I didn't see nothin' man, ya know what I saw? All I saw was funny red paint and people lying around. But I'm sittin' there and I know something is happening cause I can dig the vibrations of the people around me, ya know, who I think are very heavy, because they're my parents and all that . . . grandparents. Everything's real secure, like the . . . uh, glove compartment . . . and all of a sudden I just realized that they didn't know what was happening any more than I did. That was the first time I tasted fear.

And like this is a projection from a long way back, but I do think that, at that moment, the soul or the ghosts of those dead Indians, maybe one or two of 'em, were just running around freaking out, and just leaped into my soul, and I was like a sponge ready to just sit there and absorb it. It's not a ghost story man, it's something that really means something to me.

During a stage performance, Jim as the Dionysian reveler sang the modern myths and as the shaman he invoked a sensuous panic to make the words of the myths meaningful. He acted as if a concert were a ritual, a ceremony, a seance, and he was the medium communicating with the supernatural. He tried to shock people out of their seats, out of their ruts, out of their minds so they could view the other side of reality, if even for just a brief glimpse. His message was: break through anyway you can, but do it now. Often the message was unfocused and so it got lost in the music, the myths, the magic and the mania.

It's easy to understand why the Doors caused riots and mayhem in dozens of concert halls and auditoriums across the country. Let me recall all of the elements: Jim's strangely upsetting stage presence and his evocative, poetic language; Ray's surreal, mysterious and haunting electric keyboards; Robbie's eerie, lyrical guitar, that intoxicating combination of flamenco and bottleneck, Chuck Berry and the blues; and finally, John's primitive, sensual and exotic rhythms that unerringly followed Jim's every erratic move, and every improvised word. The audience, literally, went crazy. They become corybantian revelers, infected by divine madness. Jim called it mass hysteria in his interviews. But he was the one who incited the hysterics.

The Doors usually performed for well over an hour. When Jim was especially possessed, the only way to get him off the stage was to turn on the house lights and cut the power to his mike. If that didn't work, he would have to be carried off bodily. It happened more than once in places like Detroit, Cleveland, Chicago, New York and Philadelphia.

A Doors concert was, for most of the audience, much more than popular entertainment. It was a combination of shamanistic ceremony, religious revival, Greek tragedy, mass hallucination, Rio carnival and giant seance. Even after the band had left the stage and there was not the remotest possibility of their returning, the fans would not leave the concert hall. I saw girls touching the stage where Jim had stood and danced. In the seats there were kids too weary and dazed to move. I saw young people so wrung out emotionally that they were crying. And I saw kids with crazed eyes and beaming banjo smiles.

Backstage, meanwhile, there was either peace or pandemonium. Jim was either still possessed and not approachable, or coming down and so full of latent energy he welcomed any diversion, including the fans' requests for autographs, pictures, touches and kisses.

"There he is! Oh, Jimmy!"

"I love you, Jim."

"Sign my album, Jim . . . please."

"Smile sexy for me, Jim."

"Take a picture with me."

"Jim, Jim, Jim. Oh, Jim, please look at me!"

"Oh, please, Jim, let me kiss you, please Jim, please. . . ." He signed patiently, talked, kissed the girls, shook hands with the boys, let them take pictures of him, let them touch his hair, his hands, his body and his leather pants. They adored him.

"Sign this poster, please Jim?" a very young girl held out a poster showing Jim holding a sparkler.

"Got a pen?" he said, taking the poster and spreading it out on the wall.

"I got a Magic Marker," she replied innocently.

After a few backstage beers and the usual local media interviews, Jim and the rest of us got back into the limo that had brought us to the concert. The driver assured us that he'd have us back to our hotel in no time. As we pulled out of the backstage parking area I saw groups of young people lingering on expectantly, even now—almost two hours after the band had left the stage for the last time.

"Well, what do you think?" Jim asked, "Did we give 'em a good show?"

"Shit, yes," replied John, still high from the sheer excitment, "They were digging it. God, I mean, there was so much energy in there tonight."

"You know we made 'em wait for more than an hour," Jim remarked, "they were a good audience to wait that long."

"You gave 'em a dynamite show," someone said.

"Well, they paid their money and they deserved it," Jim replied.

"They were having a good time," Paul told Jim earnestly, "they were really getting off on it."

"Good, man! I was feeling alright, myself. I could have gone on for another hour."

"We played for an hour and a half. What more could they want?" John asked.

"Someday I'd like to just keep going. Play everything we know: blues, Elvis songs, old rock stuff. We could probably play for hours."

"Well, I doubt we'll ever get the chance. Promoters want to make their money and split." John was cynically realistic.

"That's too bad, man," Jim said, "cause I'd really like to get up there someday without a time limit and just play and sing till I dropped. Go all the way. Wouldn't that be great?"

No one answered him because no one, not even his closest friends, could imagine it.

Jim's appearance at the Hollywood Bowl in 1968 was a triumphant acclamation of the success the Doors had achieved. The cavernous Bowl was packed to capacity with fans and celebrities. Jim was never more playful, or more generous with his audience. He danced, sang, joked and recited poems. He had a good time and we captured a lot of it on film for Feast of Friends.

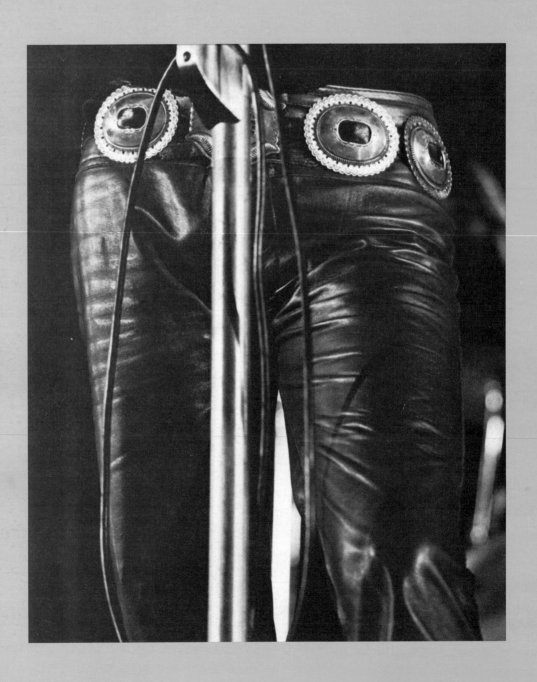

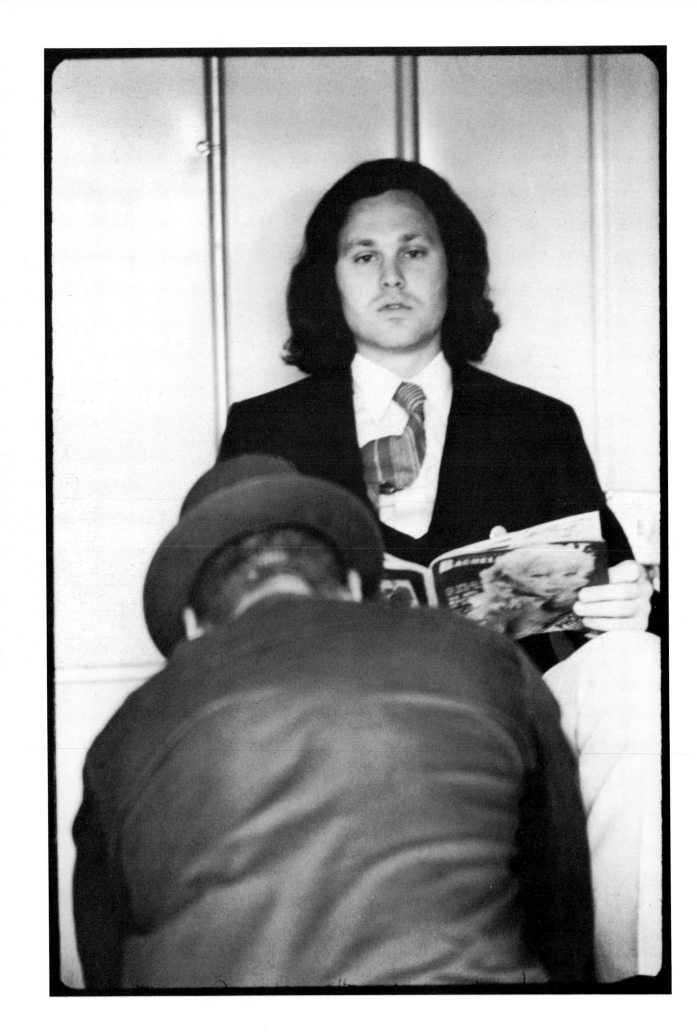

Left: Jim gets his boots shined in preparation for his trial in Phoenix.
Above: Ray and John react to?

The picture on the opposite page was taken on the first day of Jim's trial in Phoenix, Arizona. He was charged with obstructing the duties of flight personnel on a regularly scheduled airline, a federal offense. Acting on the advice of his attorney, Max Fink, Jim shaved and dressed up for his day in court. He was acquitted.

I'm a Changeling
See me change
Well, I'm the air you breathe
the food you eat
the friend you greet
in the swarming street

(JDM)

For many years, Jim was like a living mirror, reflecting whatever stood in front of him. If you looked forward to meeting Satan or a wild man, Jim could give you a good rendition of either one. If you expected Prince Charming, he could be chivalrous and dashing. Intelligent folk saw him as smart; bozos figured he was one of the bunch. Nice people knew Jim as pleasant and clowns asked him to join their circus.

Photos of Jim taken in 1967 and '68 show the face of a manly but gentle Renaissance angel. That's what the fans wanted and expected. That face was partially responsible for propelling the Doors to such great national success. The group saw their first and second albums on the charts at the same time, both albums in the top ten. Within a year of its release, "Light My Fire" had sold 1.2 million copies.

Jim's fans numbered in the millions. His stardom enhanced their ego through association and identification. He gave their existence purpose and meaning, but the fans wanted even more. They demanded a hero, a guide, a leader and a symbol. For three or four years Jim was someone to believe in, someone to hold onto during the awful emotional changes of adolescence, during bad drug trips and lonely years.

Hero worship is a normal occurrence among young people who, during adolescence, shift their respect from parents to more god-like and celebrated creatures: rock stars, film and TV personalities and professional athletes.

Jim became a symbol of youth's rebellion against the status quo, against their parents, against the war, the draft, the police, against everything they saw as wrong with America in the '60's.

Jim wrote and sang lyrics that gave his fans a way to express their deep fears, hidden feelings and terrible frustrations. When they heard the words to "Five to One," or "When the Music's Over," they said to themselves and each other, "Yeah, that's the way it is!"

They identified with Jim because he was not only their voice, but their conscience:

What have they done to the earth?
What have they done to our fair sister?
Ravaged and plundered and ripped her and bit her,
stuck her with knives in the side of the dawn,
and tied her with fences and dragged her down.
I hear a very gentle sound. . . .
With your ear down to the ground. . . .
We want the world and we want it—NOW!

WHEN THE MUSIC's OVER
(JDM)

Jim always gave you back at least as much as you gave him. He always gave a good count and never short-weighted anyone. But in the last years of his incredible life, he ceased being other people's image of him.

He changed, he developed new skills, he put on weight, grew a beard, shaved it off and grew it back again. He began to dislike performing in large halls and finally decided not to do it anymore. He became himself.

His personality and his physical appearance were not transformed for the same purpose that a chameleon changes colors to blend into the environment. Jim changed on the outside because his mind was evolving into new levels of awareness.

It was the final transition into James Douglas Morrison, Poet, that most confused and alienated his fans. They wanted him to stand still, to be forever the leather–limbed dark angel. For Jim that would have been as intolerable as wearing a mask to a fête and never again being able to remove it.

1968

1971

Most of the time Jim was so comfortable with himself, that he existed only for the moment, without anxiety about what he would need tomorrow or what he could save to recall today.

He displayed an almost un-American attitude towards the things he owned, to possessions in general, which even extended to his clothes and notebooks. Americans usually judge their own self-worth and the status of their neighbors by the amount and value of their cars, cattle, clothes, collections and cottages.

Jim never owned a house. He owned a car briefly and the total amount of other things he possessed at any one time could, and often did, fit neatly into a "carry-on" bag. He was unaffected by the attractions of ownership and I never saw him window shop. He just didn't need things, items and objects. Perhaps he considered objects real obstacles in his attempts to make the transition to the other side of reality.

If possessions were unnecessary, so was the security of a place to live. Pamela Courson, his lovely, longtime, red-haired girlfriend, tried several times to make a home for him, but Jim spent less than a fraction of his time in any one of these houses and apartments.

He preferred the anonymity of cheap motels or big hotels, an impersonal room where no one he knew could find him. Perhaps he found in these rooms a quiet, unhurried place to write, or simply a refuge from his demanding fame.

His generosity was natural and spontaneous, and he was forever giving something away. He gave me a rough-out suede, western jacket because he thought it looked good on me. He gave Kathy a rare Sioux eagle bone whistle, and he gave our friend, Babe, shirts, jackets, books, whatever was around. Jim wasn't saving for the future.

Even his journals and notebooks became excess baggage, and he left them behind in taxis, bars, restaurants and dressing rooms. Fortunately most of these journals, full of lyrics, stories, poems and observations, found their way back to him like literary homing pigeons. But he never said a word of regret about the notebooks that never flew back.

He was, at least in this one aspect, like a Zen monk. I admired, but could not emulate, his attitude.

Once when I asked him to show me the things he wrote when he was younger, he told me that he didn't have anything to show. When I pressed him for an explanation he said that a short time after leaving the UCLA Film School, he ". . . got rid . . ." of the notebooks containing his early writing. Maybe he had left them somewhere, or he could have torn out the pages and burned each one separately. All he would say was, "I was tired of carrying them around. They were just a lot of old ideas I didn't need anymore."

A writer needs the total conviction of his own potential to destroy years of work. What a refreshingly wholesome act.

Jim set an example for the life style of the sixties:

No more money, no more fancy dress....

Many people saw his disregard of material things as more reckless abandon and chaotic behavior. His freedom challenged their notion of security and values. But I can see now that he cut the binds that tie our minds and so he was able to fly.

★ ★ ★ ★ ★ ★ ★ ★ ★ ★ ★ ★ ★ ★ ★ ★ ★

Going shopping with Jim was a uniquely unsettling experience. I've always had a phobia about trying on clothes in hot, cramped dressing rooms, so I usually confine my shopping to the day after my jeans fall apart in the wash. Jim's approach was similar, but he had modified the act of purchase to fit his own unhampered needs.

One morning as I was dressing, Kathy pointed out that the boots I was about to pull on looked like they'd barely survived a long cattle drive. I examined these comfortable old friends and had to agree. They were beyond repair. It was time for a new pair of boots.

Jim was already at the Doors' office when Kathy and I arrived. He probably spent the night, as he often did, sleeping on the sofa. He greeted us with his engaging, morning-wide grin.

"Look at this," he said, handing me an airmail envelope that contained a fan letter from a young Japanese girl. Attached to her note was a handwritten poem in exquisite Emily Dickinson English.

(opposite) Kathy Lisciandro, Jim and Tony Funches.

"It's from Kame, the girl who sent you the book of poems," said Kathy as she read through the poem.

Several months before, Jim had received a notebook full of poems, handwritten in both Japanese and English, from this talented Japanese teenager. Knocked out by her trust and her poetry, Jim sent her copies of his own self-published books, *The Lords* and *The New Creatures*, along with a letter in praise of her work.

She was Jim's favorite fan, so her letter in today's mail had started his day with the fresh clarity of a clean new mirror.

"When we tour Japan, I'm going to look her up", he said. "Maybe I'll ask her to marry me. I think I'll ask her to send me a picture. Should I send her a picture of me?"

"I'm sure she knows what you look like, Jim". Kathy was always reasonable.

I can only imagine what a dazzling East-West word garden these two poets could have planted had they ever met. Unfortunately, the Doors never toured Japan.

Kathy had already opened the morning mail and was calling the answering service for last night's messages. Any minute now we could expect the arrival of Bill Siddons, Leon Barnard, Vince Treanor or some crazy from off the street. It was time to leave the office.

"Hey, man, I'm going to go buy some new boots, wanna come for a ride?"

"Yeah . . . I might buy new boots, too."

Jim checked his schedule with Kathy and they decided there wasn't anything he couldn't miss.

So we drove across the Hollywood hills into the hot valley on the other side, twirling the radio dial, listening for anything that sounded new or something old. We talked about Japan, its people, culture, arts, films and women.

I had decided to look for boots at a western clothing and saddle shop that Bill Doherty, a friend from film school days, had told me about. It was a Texas-size emporium that sold everything from 10 and 12 gallon hats to horse blankets, western shirts, silver–studded bridles and belt buckles, and a whole department devoted to western style boots.

Jim wandered around the store while I struggled to pull on and off a variety of styles and sizes. I chose an ochre colored pair made by Justin, with soft calf leather uppers, showing a minimum of tooling.

I threw my comfortable old friends in the box the new ones came out of. As I was counting out the bucks for the boots, I saw Jim emerging from a dressing stall. He was wearing new socks, a new black T-shirt and new western cut black cotton slacks. He carried the clothes he had been wearing over to the boot department where he spent less than thirty seconds eyeing the vast selection. Without hesitation he chose a pair of plain, but solid, black boots with square toes. When the young salesman emerged from the storeroom with a large square box, Jim took out the boots, pulled them on his feet, stood up, walked a few paces and said, "I'll take these".

"Do you want to keep 'em on?" asked the salesman.

"Yeah, I'll wear 'em."

"OK, I'll wrap up your old ones for you."

"No, man, just throw them away or burn 'em," Jim told him. "The same with all this other stuff." He pointed to the pile of clothing he had been wearing when he came into the store.

"You . . . you sure you don't want any of this stuff?" The young man was rattled.

"Oh, yeah, wait a minute." Jim searched through the pockets of his discarded pants, pulling out a plastic credit card, the Doors' office key and his folded and torn California driver's license.

"Thanks," said Jim.

"Yeah, sure . . . ." replied the bewildered salesman, who finally just shook his head and walked away.

Jim paid for the new clothes with his plastic money, carefully showing the cashier everything he had on and telling her the price of each item, including the socks.

We left the store and walked into the blinding, blinking sunlight reflected off pavement, storefront windows and passing cars. Jim had changed his skin again. I had seen him do it, but it had happened so quickly I couldn't even recall what he was wearing when we entered the store.

He saw me staring at him and asked, "Well, what d'ya wanna do now?"

"How about short haircuts?" I replied.

He put his head into the thirty degree angle he favored when studying a person or new idea. He seemed to be seriously evaluating my facetious suggestion. I could picture us walking into the office with short hair, maybe even flat tops. No one was going to think it was funny. They'd probably blame me. I ran my hand through my shoulder length hair.

Jim smiled, and said with young boy earnestness, "Let's save it for another day."

"Well, OK . . . but you sure you wouldn't like a new face to go with your new threads?" I knew I was carrying the joke too far but I couldn't stop myself. Maybe the combination of the smog and the hot San Fernando Valley sun was frying my brains. I looked around for air conditioned shade.

Jim had the same idea. "Come on, man, let's get out of this heat and into a cold beer before you talk me into something I'll regret. The biggest mistakes in my life have been haircuts."

As we walked to the car our stiff new boots sounded like synchronized sledge hammers.

"They're sure gonna know we're coming," I said.

"Yeah," Jim said, "no more sneaking around for me for awhile."

LIGHT MY FIRE

When The Doors performed "Light My Fire" on WNET-TV, New York City in 1970, I tried to capture Jim's dynamic performance on film. The photo on this page picks up the song just before the guitar and keyboard instrumental break. (opposite) Jim encourages Ray.

Try to set the night on fire,
Try to set the night on fire.

Jim listens and waits while Robbie and Ray exchange solos.

The time to hesitate is through,
No time to wallow in the mire
Try now we can only lose,
And our love become a funeral pyre.

Come on baby, light my fire
Come on baby, light my fire
Try to set the night on fire.
Try to set the night on fire.

You know that it would be untrue;
You know that I would be a liar;
If I was to say to you;
Girl, we couldn't get much higher;

Come on baby, light my fire
Come on baby, light my fire
Try to set the night on fire,
Try to set the night on fire,
Try to set the night on fire,
Try to set the night on fire.

Jim caps "Light My Fire" with a smashing drum accent.

By mid-1969 the Doors were firmly entrenched as the number one American rock 'n' roll band. Their first three albums had gone gold and each of their nine singles climbed its way up the charts. They were commanding big bucks to appear before vast crowds in concert halls, auditoriums and sports arenas from California to the shores of the Atlantic.

Jim's name and face had national recognition and the press was always ready to report his more outrageous escapades. *Life* magazine ran an article about the Doors and their music, complete with photos of the police busting Jim and dragging him off the stage in New Haven, Connecticut. The writer could find no justification for the arrest; just another example of Jim enraging the uptight sensibilities of the local guardians of authority and morality.

In March of 1969 Jim was charged with, among other things, indecent exposure during a performance in a hot and vastly overcrowded auditorium in Miami. Newspapers, wire services and rock magazines told the world about it and most people concluded that he had indeed flashed his cock in concert. Because he was a public figure who advocated freedom, he was presumed guilty from the start. Fame had turned from laurel wreath to millstone.

Despite the triumphs and the troubles, Jim managed to keep his sense of humor. He relished danger, fun and adventure. As soon as life in L.A. started to become burdensome or predictable, he would seize any opportunity to get away. When no legitimate excuse presented itself, he would simply disappear for a few days or weeks.

In May of 1969, a telegram from the Atlanta International Film Festival provided Jim with a way out of L.A. The Festival, honoring *Feast of Friends* with a Gold Medal, had extended an invitation to the filmmakers to pick up the award.

When Jim asked me to accompany him to Atlanta, I accepted without hesitation. I was just as itchy to be on the road as he was, and I wanted to see Jim in a setting that would be difficult for him to dominate and relatively immune to his pre-established fame. He had recently grown a beard so that for the first time in his career he was virtually unrecognizable.

We threw a change of clothes and a selection of books in "carry-on" bags and left for the airport. We were very late and as we were rushed to the boarding ramp in an airline electric cart, it suddenly occurred to me that Jim was always missing or almost missing planes. Paranoia, induced, no doubt, by racing too fast through jet fumes, seized control. Was Fate trying to warn Jim not to fly? Could it be that he was destined to die in a flaming crash and his subconscious mind was trying to hinder him from getting on planes? It could happen at any time, even on this flight!

All of a sudden the trip to Atlanta lost its appeal. Jim noticed me turning pale and holding on, white-knuckled, to the tube frame of the electric cart that was speeding us towards our departure gate.

"Don't worry, man. We'll make it. They'll hold the plane," he said.

It was not exactly the reassurance I wanted, but of course he was right; they did hold the plane.

After a few drinks I began to lose the creepy feeling of impending doom, and somewhere over Texas my first experience with fear of flight had evaporated. When I told Jim about my delusion, he looked out the window before he said, "I wouldn't mind dying in a plane crash. It would be a good way to go".

"A good way as compared to what?" I asked.

"I just don't want to die of old age or O.D. or drift off in my sleep." He seemed to have given the subject serious consideration.

"Dying in your sleep seems like the most pleasant and least painful way."

"Yeah, but you don't get to experience anything, you just slip right into it. I want to feel what it's like. I want to taste it, hear it, smell it. Death is only going to happen once, right? I don't want to miss it."

"What's to experience? Your whole life flashing by in single frame cuts? I could do without it."

"Don't knock it if you haven't tried it", he said.

We landed without my having to review my encapsulated life at high speed. At the Festival headquarters we were greeted by Mr. J. Hunter Todd, the head honcho, who was delighted, even thrilled, to have Jim to show off. Jim and I were equally delighted with Hunter's attache case which contained a built-in mobile phone, the first we had ever seen. Jim had to try it, placing calls to L.A. (no one was in), and to an Atlanta D.J. Jim asked him to please announce the next day's showing of *Feast of Friends*. The D.J. immediately put Jim on the air to make the announcement himself via the mobile phone.

Although the film was screened in the middle of the day, the theater was almost filled. During the fourteen-minute rendition of "The End", which climaxes *Feast*, not one person in the audience moved. Jim's face in close-up was almost eight feet high on the theater screen. Following his eyes and straining to hear his every word, the audience seemed spellbound.

For me, watching the film with this enthusiastic audience, was almost like seeing it fresh, for the first time. I was swept up in the emotional response to the songs and images. Accidents of juxtaposition and the hard–edged documentary reality gave the film a vibrant urgency.

After the lights came up, Jim was introduced and speedily surrounded by fans. Most just wanted to stand and stare; some asked questions: "How do you like Atlanta, Jim?"; "Why is the band called the Doors?"; "Did you ever meet the Beatles?". . . . The bolder girls ventured close enough to touch him.

Jim endured it all good naturedly: the frivolous questions, the requests for autographs, the touches. Many people asked to see the film again, while others wanted the Doors to "please play" in Atlanta.

Jim came away with his pockets full of invitations, phone numbers and addresses.

That night Jim and I wandered down to what had been described to us as Atlanta's "hippie" section. We were invited to a rent party in one of the older Victorian houses which was inhabited by college students, runaways, street people, artists, musicians, army deserters: the whole spectrum of a '60's commune environment. Jim was treated with universal reverence, and I was assumed to be a member of the Doors, hence a lesser deity.

The young people in Atlanta seemed much more conservative in lifestyle and appearance in comparison to the West Coast, where people dressed in fanciful, colorful clothes that made them resemble pirates, princesses, gypsies, clowns, bikers, magicians, cowboys, Edwardian fops, Indians and Hindu gurus. At this party, men wore jeans and work shirts or T-shirts, while the ladies dressed as if they had never heard of Carnaby Street. Grass was passed around furtively, while tales were told of constant police harassment.

In contrast to his arrogant, cool, distant and wild stage stance, Jim was open, approachable, funny and friendly with these young fans. A circle of girls, almost like a protective shield, sat on the floor at his feet. He seemed completely at ease, comfortable and natural. When a collection was taken for a beer run, he slipped a $20 bill in the pot and even offered to help carry the booze back to the house. He was undemanding and helpful, the perfect guest. I cracked up watching him help out in the kitchen, preparing snacks. He picked out albums, changed records, passed out beers and listened to complaints about cops, school and parents. He did not offer advice, but he shared his own similar experiences. His presence at the party, and especially his no-bullshit lack of pretentions, conveyed a total equality. It was like he was one of them and his fame was theirs to share, because he spoke for them.

Did he really represent the attitudes of fourteen to twenty-five year olds all over the country? And if he did, was it the well-spring of his anger and belligerence toward society? Could these young people who admired him be a source of his power?

Jim wasn't so cooperative the next night at the Awards ceremony banquet, though. We had not been told that the event was formal and even if we had, Jim would not have changed his leather pants and suede jacket for a tux and bow tie.

More than 400 people sat at eight–place tables in the enormous banquet room of the Hyatt Regency Hotel. As we were led to our table, 800 eyes followed us, signalling a mixture of curiosity and disapproval. I was hoping that we would be seated at an unoccupied table in a corner so that we would not have to make small talk with these dressed–up folk who were obviously twice our age and more than a little upset at our appearance.

Instead, we were placed at a table near the center of the room already occupied with other award winners. We introduced ourselves and Jim, in a magnanimous gesture, ordered six bottles of Pouilly-Fuisse to be shared by our fellow diners.

The first course brought a vivid portent of what a disaster the meal would be. My soup was watery and disagreeably flavored. Jim didn't bother to taste his. Instead, he emptied his water tumbler into the soup bowl and proceeded to fill it with the excellent French white wine. The big water glass held more than a third of the bottle. To the woman across the table who watched him, Jim explained, "I never eat soup."

He didn't touch any of the other courses either, but kept filling his water glass with wine. For the most part, table conversation swirled around us, but whenever Jim was asked a direct question, he answered with non-sequiturs, or funny one-line remarks:

"Where are you young men from?" the woman on my right asked us in a sweet drawl.

"From the top, ma'am," Jim said, pointing his finger and lifting his eyes.

Although he never said anything mean, Jim's remarks were interpreted as derisive. He was trying to poke holes in the puffed–up vanity of our fellow awardees, but it wasn't working.

The only unpleasant person at the table was a middle-aged guy who claimed he produced TV commercials in Florida.

"I guess no one told you boys that this wasn't a rock concert," he began as soon as we sat down. He wanted to know if our film was "x-perri-mental." He pronounced the word as if it denoted an incurable brain disease.

"I've seen 'x-perri-mental' films from that fella Brakage, and I didn't get anything out of it but a headache."

"Serves you right," Jim muttered, but our antagonist was still talking and didn't hear him.

"You fellas make films like that, hard on the eyes?"

I was feeling feisty and full of wine, so I decided to take him on. I asked him what camera and film stock he used to shoot his commercials and whether he preferred the stock pre-flashed or post-flashed and were his crews IATSE or NABET.

He didn't know what I was talking about. His confusion and lack of technical knowledge were apparent to everyone at that table.

"I hire boys who know that technical stuff. I know what sells!" he replied. "And I don't show up at a banquet with dirty clothes. . . . " He was ready to go on in this vein but his wife, a lady of not insignificant size, hushed him, and I decided to ignore him.

Jim was never impolite, but he became incoherent after three water tumblers of wine. I was so shockingly drunk that I had real trouble sitting balanced on my chair. A part of my brain kept nagging me to remember something, but a sweet fog had settled in my memory.

What I had forgotten all evening was that one of us was going to have to get up to accept the award. In fact, the awards portion of the banquet had already started and was proceeding on the dais. I could see it clearly in double vision.

I think I moaned out loud. Everyone at the table, except Jim, must have interpreted this to mean I was going to be sick because there was a sudden retreating of chairs from my general vicinity. Jim looked at me, his eyes at half mast, and gave me a lopsided, engaging smile.

"Ain't this great?" is what I think he said, but between his slurred speech and my alcohol–impaired hearing, he could have said anything.

"You gotta get our award," I managed to say. He started to get up.

"Not now." I pulled him down.

"You go get it," he said. "You did it." He searched through the wine bottles, but they were, by this time, all empty.

"No . . . you have to get it, man," I said, "I can't. . . . "

"OK, OK, but you should, really. . . . "

It was going to be a toss-up for disaster for whoever got up to get it.

The attention of everyone else in the room was now firmly focused on the dais where lovely young ladies in low-cut gowns were handing plaques and certificates to an endless stream of grinning filmmakers. Jim, realizing that no one was paying the slightest bit of attention to him, grabbed an empty wine bottle, shoved it under the draping, white table cover, unzipped his fly and enjoyed the relief of emptying his bursting bladder. Finished, he returned the now almost filled green wine bottle to the table, placing it among the empty ones.

I don't think anyone noticed Jim's unique urination, but I began to worry about that full wine bottle. I thought it would be a safe idea to get it off the table and was about to tell Jim so when I heard the MC announce our award.

Jim jumped to his feet and stood swaying next to the table, holding on with his fingertips, trying to regain balance and equilibrium. I was trying to get to my feet to lend a hand, but before I could rise, he lurched off, shuffling and stumbling through the maze of tables.

On the dais, a devastatingly cute and voluptuous girl handed Jim a gaudy black and silver plaque. Jim gave her his room key in return. After being subjected to near blinding by the strobe-happy Awards photographer, Jim kissed the cutie and came back to the table, beaming from ear to ear, the plaque tucked under his arm.

A few minutes later, as we were leaving the banquet, I noticed the TV commercial producer from Florida reaching for the only full wine bottle on the table. I stopped to watch. He grabbed the bottle and as he lifted it to his glass, a montage of reactions flickered across his face, 24 frames per second. He went from surprise at the bottle's warmth, to bafflement, to reluctant realization, to disgust, to anger, to rage, to. . . . I didn't stay to see the rest.

I caught up with Jim and told him about it as we exited, mimicking as best I could the guy's facial expressions. We stopped at the door and laughed so hard that the enormous room full of people turned to stare. Jim waved the plaque at them and we left. I'm sure they thought we were both certified loonies and probably very dangerous dudes.

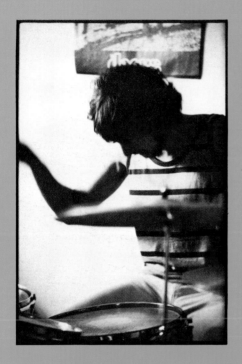

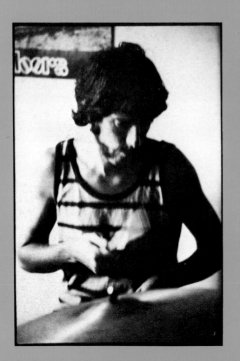
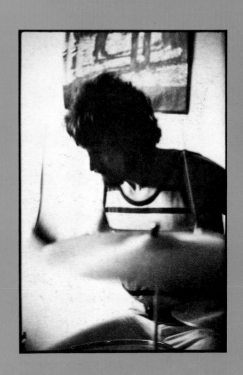

The morning after the awards banquet I was shocked to see two bleary, bloodshot eyes, supported by crescent shadows, peering back at me from the morning mirror. My skin was pale and my head was pounding in 7/4 time.

I was trying to get interested in a plate of easy-over eggs, bacon, whole wheat toast and grits, when Jim joined me in the hotel coffee shop. He was fresh and lively as a kitten, smiling and bouncy.

"You look awful, man," he said, but I already knew that. "You shouldn't eat that stuff, it'll make you sick."

He called over the waiter and ordered us each a Ramos Gin Fizz.

"You'll feel a lot better after a couple of these," he promised, "and later you'll be able to eat lunch."

The Ramos was cold and delicious and I felt less sick after absorbing a tall one. At the first sign of my improved condition, Jim began his pitch.

"Hey, man, I've been thinking. Since we're so close, how about going to New Orleans for a few days before we head back to L.A."

"OK by me. When do you want to go?"

"Let's go today, this morning," he said.

The second Ramos Gin Fizz got my blood surging and my headache mysteriously disappeared.

"Do you think we can get plane tickets?" I was feeling much better.

"I'd rather drive," he said.

"You wanna drive to New Orleans?"

"Sure . . . you don't get to see anything from the air. We'll rent a car and split the driving."

"Are you kidding, man? You wanna drive through the deep South looking the way we do? Didn't you ever see *Easy Rider*?"

"The people in the South are gracious and hospitable. I should know, man, I grew up here."

Jim grew up in Alexandria, Virginia; Clearwater, Florida; Albuquerque, New Mexico; Alameda, California; Washington, D.C. and three or four other places, but I let him slide on that one.

"It's a hell of a long way to drive."

"Five hundred miles. What d'ya say?" He was leaving the decision to me. He looked like a little boy asking to be taken to the amusement park. He had on his patented half grin and his eyes sparkled with mischief.

"You ever been there?" he asked me.

"No, never. Have you?"

"Not yet."

"OK, man, but if we're going to drive we had best be cool."

"Right", he agreed.

We checked out of the hotel, threw our two small bags in an air-conditioned rental Ford, and were on the open road in less than an hour. I was torn between my love of travel and the thought of what might be out there, waiting beside some swamp for two smart-ass hippie types. 1969 was not a year of good press for long hair and beards. The hippies had ruined the image.

The countryside was pastoral and Jim commented on everything, like a new soul in the universe, seeing everything fresh for the first time, but knowing everything too.

"Look at that tree with Spanish moss on it. It's a cottonwood. Might be two hundred years old. You can't see it but the moss is made up of millions of delicate flowers. It's ironic, but it will eventually kill the tree."

As we drove we talked about our lives. He was interested in my stories about growing up on the tough streets of Brooklyn, with gangs, rumbles and street corner acappella groups. We both agreed that rock 'n' roll, the most influential social statement of our teenage years, stopped with the death of Buddy Holly in '59, and didn't start up again until the Beatles led the English invasion in '63. After the fireworks ignited by originals like Buddy Holly, Elvis, Chuck Berry, Jerry Lee Lewis, Little Richard, Gene Vincent and Fats Domino, the air waves were lost to the baby-faced mushy romantics.

"That's when I discovered the Blues," Jim told me. He explained that the Blues were one of the few truly original American art forms. "Rock 'n' Roll," he said, "was a mixed breed" . . . born of the Blues, which had its origins in Africa and in the country and mountain music that originally came from Scotland, Ireland and England.

"Rock 'n' Roll is a perfect mix of white music and black music and that's why I love it."

He also loved America, despite its faults.

"I really feel at home here, man, in America. To me, America is like a warm neon breast. When I'm away from this country it's like an expedition."

We discovered a common ground in the Beat writers and poets and especially in Jack Kerouac's *On The Road*, the book that fueled our generation's desire to see America non-stop from a fast car. Jim loved the way Dean Moriarity spoke in quick, condensed jazz cadence, like a scat singer:

"Oh man, what kicks!" yelled Dean. "Now Marylou, listen really, honey, you know that I'm hotrock capable of everything at the same time and I have unlimited energy —now in San Francisco we must go on living together. I know just the place for you—at the end of the regular chain-gang run—I'll be home just a cut - hair less than every two days and for twelve hours at a stretch, and man, you know what we can do in twelve hours, darling. Meanwhile I'll go right on living at Camille's like nothin, see, she won't know. We can work it, we've done it before."

Our heroes drove at night along highways that rolled on forever. They stopped at dawn in little roadside cafes for coffee and donuts. The cool image was represented by James Dean: dark sunglasses, worn all the time; dark slacks; a leather or suede sports coat; a vacant stare and nothing at all to smile about. It was the only truly indelible romantic look of the '50's and it had hooked both of us.

This drive was a little like trying to recapture that spirit. We stopped often for cold Cokes at roadside stores. The people we encountered regarded us with mild curiousity, but without hostility. The towns we sped through were sleepy, run down and left behind by the rush of technology.

"The South is down at the mouth," was Jim's summation.

The two-lane county roads brought us past shanty towns and tar paper shacks that had barely survived the last heavy rain storm. We were stunned by the level of poverty and deprivation. I never expected to see people living this poorly in the U.S.A. Jim's sense of justice was outraged.

"Somebody's going to pay for this someday," was all he said. We drove on in angry silence.

We arrived in New Orleans with the sun and headed straight for the French Quarter and found a hotel. After a patio breakfast, we spent the rest of the morning and half of the afternoon in our rooms, reading, writing and sleeping. By six p.m. we were out on the streets, exploring the town's rich texture and diversity. Jim often said, "I want to experience everything at least once." New Orleans was filled to the brim with opportunities.

We had a look in almost every club, bar and cafe we passed. In a few we stayed for drinks. We met Norwegian sailors, Australian scientists, dope dealers, housewives, hookers, musicians, taxi drivers . . . it seemed as if the town were populated with characters waiting to be cast in a Tennessee Williams play.

After dinner, starting about midnight, we sampled the musical pleasures of the clubs on and around Bourbon St. By four a.m. we were still going strong, energized and enlivened by the music, the damp, cool night air and the exuberance of the crowds in the clubs. We didn't get back to the hotel until 5:30. Behind us New Orleans was still shaking and partying.

The next day was hot, humid and overcast. Since we had started out from Los Angeles with only a single change of clothes, our first concern was finding something fresh to wear. We stopped at a shop close to the hotel, where we changed into tie-dyed T-shirts and lightweight slacks. Jim made the acquaintance of Jill, a sweet, lively and humorous lady who told us she was the store manager and graciously offered to have our dirty clothes washed and ironed. When we asked about places to hear rock 'n' roll, she said she'd take us to a club. Her good looks, charm and generosity knocked Jim off his feet and I finally had to drag him out of the store.

"You know, I think she likes me." He delighted in being bearded, anonymous and unannounced.

I knew Jim was bound to blow his cover the minute we walked into the rock club that night. The band was playing blues-based R & B, not too different from the kind of sound made by Canned Heat. Jim listened, itching to get up on stage. Between sets he approached the band and asked if he could sing. They said

sure thing and handed him the mike. After a short conference about what song and what key he wanted to sing in, the band started playing John Lee Hooker's classic, "Crawling King Snake." Jim listened, the mike in one hand, his head down, eyes closed, and his foot tapping time. He stayed that way for twenty or thirty seconds. The band members started exchanging glances that said, "What's this cat going to do?" Finally, when Jim could feel that the band had settled into a nice steady groove, he opened his eyes, licked his lips, smiled at the audience and began to sing. He was in great voice, using all the experience he had developed over the last three years to nurse, stroke and rock the lyrics.

Jill, from the clothes store, sparkled with smiles. Part of the audience was riveted to the song, while another part buzzed with excited curiosity. I heard "Morrison" whispered a few times along with other names. No one was really sure who this bearded blues singer was. At the end of the song the audience asked for more. Jim obliged them with another blues number, "Little Red Rooster," this time making up words and whole stanzas to elongate and personalize the song. He improvised with such surety that the original words seemed dull and predictable in comparison. I had never heard him sing like this before; I had rarely heard him sing as good. It wasn't at all like a Doors concert: the theater, ritual, and dark, strange corners were missing. This was just pure entertaining fun.

The band played their asses off because Jim made them sound great. After two more numbers he put the mike back on the stand, thanked the band and returned to our table. The guitar player had questioned Jim between songs and now announced to the audience that it had been a great pleasure to make music with Jim Morrison of the Doors. The audience cheered, applauded and asked for more, but Jim firmly resisted their entreaties. Good show biz tactic, Jimbo, I thought to myself, always leave 'em wanting more.

The next afternoon, as we strolled around the French Quarter, we came upon Rudolf Nureyev, the ballet star. He was alone and also occupying his time with sightseeing. Jim and I debated if it would be cool to say hello to him. We realized that this might be the only opportunity we'd ever have, so why not seize it?

Nureyev is of medium height, slender, with a strong Slavic face and deep penetrating eyes. He walked with the grace of a Fred Astaire, head straight, feet lightly touching the ground. He was friendly, unbothered by two long hairs stopping him to say hello. He was not familiar with Jim's name or the Doors and confessed general ignorance about the whole subject of rock 'n' roll.

I stood a little apart to watch these two men who were equally as famous in their own art form and equally as gifted. I was sure many Doors' fans had never heard of Nureyev, but Jim seemed genuinely star struck.

The ballet dancer asked Jim if he was a famous singer and Morrison admitted that, in a way, he was.

"You have a big beard, like old Russians," Nureyev told Jim, "it is a good way to hide, no?"

Jim laughed and said that his beard was indeed a good disguise.

"I can not grow such a beard," Nureyev said. "You would never see a ballet dancer with a beard." We all laughed at that mental image.

We walked a little way along the street together and Jim asked if he ever got homesick for Russia.

"All the time," Nureyev admitted, "but I am learning to like America, now."

Too soon it was time for him to rejoin the troupe for that evening's performance and time for us to get back to the hotel to pack.

I told Jim that I thought it was strange that Nureyev could walk along the streets in daylight, alone, without any attempt at disguise, and not be pestered, bothered and molested by fans and admirers.

"It's a different audience entirely," Jim replied. "Nureyev's audience attends out of aesthetic appreciation and intellectual enjoyment. But the popular arts like rock excite more visceral responses. People get all worked up. I guess that's why rock appeals more to younger people who are more easily excitable."

"Would you rather appeal to the ballet crowd?"

"No, man, kids are the future. And kids you can change and mold and influence. That's what's important about a young audience. They're like clean paper waiting to be written on."

"And you're the pen?" I teased.

"No, man, I'm the ink!" he laughed.

★ ★ ★ ★ ★ ★ ★ ★ ★ ★ ★ ★ ★ ★ ★ ★ ★ ★

We arrived in Los Angeles late that night and Jim went to stay at Pamela's house in the Hollywood hills. He returned to the busy existence of recording studios, concerts, business meetings and rehearsals, once again a prisoner of his own device. For a few days he had busted out to freedom and this trip, more than anything else, cemented our friendship and mutual admiration. Even for a confirmed solo traveller like myself, Jim was a good companion: easy to get along with, humorous, never complaining, considerate and always ready to accept the unexpected.

We both had, as the Southern California '60's expression put it, "a bitchin' good time."

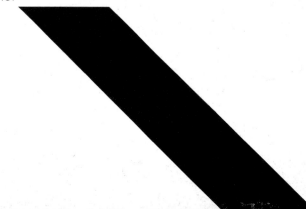

Albert King and Jim after the show, Vancouver, 1970.

Jim performs at the Aquarius Theater, Los Angeles, 1969.

WHISKEY, MYSTICS AND MEN

Well, I'll tell you a story of whiskey and mystics and men,
And about the believers and how the whole thing began.
First there were women and children obeying the moon,
Then daylight brought wisdom and fever and sickness too soon.
You can try to remind me instead of the other, you can.
You can help to insure that we all insecure our command.
If you don't give a listen, I won't try to tell your new hand.
This is it; can't you see that we all have our ends in the band.
And if all of the teachers and preachers of wealth were arraigned,
We could see quite a future for me in the literal sands.
And if all of the people could claim to inspect such regrets,
Well, we'd have no forgiveness, forgetfullness, faithful remorse.
So I tell you, I tell you, I tell you we must send away.
We must try to find a new answer instead of a way.

(JDM)

sounds of the fire
(whistles, rattlesnakes, castanets)

< I am the Lizard King
I can do anything
I can make the earth stop in its tracks
I made the blue cars go away

For seven years I dwelt
in the loose palace of exile,
Playing strange games
w/ the girls of the island.

Now I have come again
To the land of the fair, & the strong, & the wise.

Brothers & sisters of the pale forest
O children of Night
Who among you will run w/ the hunt?

Now Night arrives w/ her purple legion,
Retire now to your tents & to your dreams.
Tomorrow we enter the Town of my birth.
I want to be ready. ⅂

Rehearsals for most of The Doors' albums were held in a room on the ground floor of a building at 8512 Santa Monica Blvd. in West Hollywood. Upstairs, Bill Siddons conducted business for the band while downstairs, in a large and littered space, the group pieced together their songs. Jim never noticed the unpainted walls and dirty carpet because, for him, the room was a laboratory where he could mix his words and his voice with the sounds of the band's instruments. The Doors' seventh Elektra album began with Jim reading his poems and lyrics to the band. Sometimes, Jim would already have a melody or rhythm worked out but, more often, the music was made from the spontaneous contributions of Robbie, Ray and John. After enough material for an album had been crafted and practiced, Paul Rothchild, who had produced all of the The Doors' previous albums, was called in to listen to the songs. In the photograph on page 99, Jim demonstrates the rhythmic feeling he wants for ''Been Down So Long'' to Robbie and Paul.

L.A. WOMAN: *REHEARSAL*

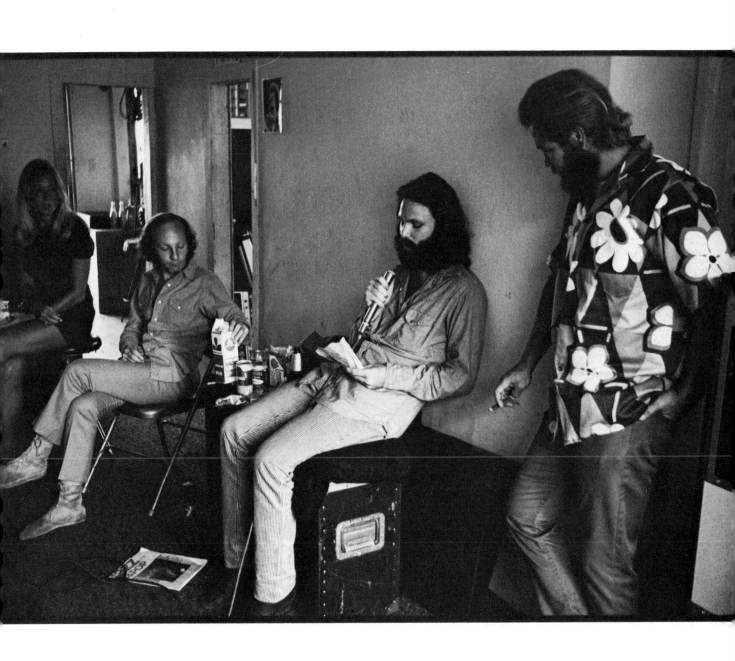

From left to right: Ray, John, Cheri Siddons, Paul Rothchild, Jim and Babe Hill.

Paul Rothchild left rehearsal early. He didn't like the songs and he thought the playing was ragged.

DRY WATER

The velvet fur of religion
The polish of knife handle & coin
The universe of organic gears
or microscope mechanical
embryo metal doll
The night is a steel machine
grinding its slow stained wheels
The brain is filled w/clocks, & drills
& water down drains
Knife-handle, thick blood
like the coin & cloth
they rub & the skin they love
to touch

the graveyard, the tombstone,
the gloomstone & runestone
The sand & the moon, mating
deep in the western night
waiting for the escape
of one of our gang
The hangman's noose is a
silver sluice bait
come-on man
your meat is hanging
on the wing of the raven
man's bird, poet's soul

Shhhhhhhhhhhhh
the thin rustle of weeds
the voice comes from faraway
inside, awaiting its birth
in a cool room, on tendril bone
The insane free chummy cackle
of infants in a ballroom, of a
family of friends around
a table, laden w/feast-food
soft guilty female laughter
the bar-room, the men's room
people assemble to establish
armies & find their foe
& fight

(JDM)

111

The Doors were demoralized by Paul Rothchild's decision not to produce the last album they owed Elektra Records. The completion of the album was vital to Jim because it meant freedom from his obligations to the band and to the record company. He set out to convince Robbie, Ray and John that they could produce the record themselves, and in their own studio. Jim's arguments swayed them, and soon the dingy downstairs rehearsal room on Santa Monica Blvd. was transformed into a funky but functional sound studio. A jukebox, pinball machine and old sofa were added, and Bruce Botnik moved a recording console and tape deck into the upstairs offices. Jerry Scheff and Marc Benno were hired to play bass and rhythm guitar. The album that resulted from these sessions was a tremendous popular success and contained two classic Morrison songs, "Riders On The Storm," and the title track, "L.A. Woman."

Jim sings, "Been Down So Long," while Marc Benno, Ray and Robbie play guitars.

The 1st electric wildness came
over the people
on sweet Friday.
Sweat was in the air.
The channel beamed,
token of power.
Incense brewed darkly.
Who could tell then that here
it would end?

One school bus crashed w/a train.
This was the Crossroads.
Mercury strained.
I couldn't get out of my seat.
The road was littered
w/dead jitterbugs.
Help,
we'll be late for class.

The secret flurry of rumor
marched over the yard &
pinned us unwittingly.
Mt. fever.
A girl stripped naked on the
base of the flagpole.

In the restrooms all was cool
& silent
w/the salt-green of latrines.
Blankets were needed.

Ropes fluttered.
Smiles flattered
& haunted.
Lockers were pryed open
& secrets discovered.

Ah sweet music.
Wild sounds in the night
Angel siren voices.
The baying of great hounds.
Cars screaming thru gears
& shrieks
on the wild road
Where the tires skid & slide
into dangerous curves.

Favorite corners.
Cheerleaders raped in summer
buildings.
Holding hands
& bopping toward Sunday.
Those lean sweet desperate hours.

Time searched the hallways
for a mind.
Hands kept time.
The climate altered like a
visible dance.

Night-time women.
Wondrous sacraments of doubt
sprang sullen in bursts
of fear & guilt
in the womb's pit hole
below
The belt of the beast.

*There are continents & shores
which beseech our understanding*

(JDM)

It was already past midnight and the chill October night was heavy with the threat of an early Midwest snowstorm.

The concert was definitely over. The audience was being persuaded by the cops to go home. The MC came out to say that the Doors were not going to come back for a third encore. The announcement was met with chants: "We want Jim!" "We want Jim!"

At that moment, Jim, together with Ray, Robbie, John and various friends and members of the press, were enjoying beers in the large backstage dressing room. As the chanting ebbed, two pretty teenage girls were led to the open dressing room by an overweight, middle-aged city cop. He acted like he might be a relative or neighbor, equally protective and annoyed.

The cop approached the oversized college jock the promoters had hired to stand guard and explained that the girls wanted autographs. Now the college guy had been instructed to let no one inside, especially not fans wanting autographs, but he didn't know what to do when faced with a symbol of authority greater than his own. So he looked around for help.

Jim had noticed the confrontation, and sensing a little fun, went out to meet his fans. The young lovelies, seeing Jim approach, began making soft, involuntary sounds: "Oooh . . . oh, no . . . it's him! . . . oh, gawd . . . aaah . . . ." As he got closer, the girls started taking small steps backward.

The cop looked at the girls, looked at Jim, looked back at the girls and ended up looking confused.

"You in the group?" he demanded.

"Yeah, I'll sign those." Jim took a pen and scraps of paper from the cop and smiled at the still retreating nymphs who were now blushing vividly, squirming and trying not to pee in their pants.

"What're your names?" Jim asked them. They stammered out their names in genuine embarrassment.

"What?" Jim laughed, taking a step toward them. They were now melting under his mesmerizing smile.

"This one's Nancy," the cop said, pointing, "and the other one's Sheila. She's my niece."

The girls, awash in conflicting emotions, held onto each other for support, while Jim wrote on each of the slips of paper.

"I don't know what's wrong with 'em. They ain't usually this shy."

Jim reached out to hand the slips of paper to his two fans when the one named Nancy screwed up her courage, whipped out an Instamatic, and demurely asked, "Could I . . . please, take a picture of you, Jim? Please?"

She lifted the camera to her eye, pointed it at Jim, ready to shoot no matter what his answer might be. Jim held his hand out, palm raised toward the lens.

"Hey, wait a minute. This guy's a professional photographer," he said, indicating me. "Let's have him take a picture of the three of us." Nancy quickly handed the camera to me and Jim gave me the pen and the autographed pieces of paper.

He posed with one arm grasping each of them firmly. They were ready to faint. The cop strutted and beamed like he had arranged a meeting with the Pope.

I hate Instamatics. If they don't work, I don't know why, and if they do work, I can't figure out how. I lined up the three smiling figures in the viewfinder, said the appropriate Kodak prayer, pushed the button and the flash went off.

The girls were shocked into immobility and would have stood there frozen in Jim's embrace for all eternity if the cop hadn't been in a hurry to get to his favorite tavern and boast of his avuncular deed.

"Come on, girls, thank the man and let's get home. It's late enough."

The sweet young things started to make those soft, sighing sounds again. I handed the camera back to Nancy and portioned out the slips of paper Jim had written on. It was then that I noticed what he had written: "To Nancy, Love Arthur Rimbaud" and "To Sheila, Love Arthur Rimbaud."

I glanced at him and he raised his eyebrows conspiratorally, then with a sweet, "Bye, Nancy," "Bye, Sheila," he went back into the dressing room.

The lovelies were led away by their uncle,

the cop, too stunned to read or even glance at the autographs. After all, hadn't they touched him and didn't they have a photo with his arms around them to prove it to their friends?

Nancy, Sheila: if that photo turned out good, I'd sure love to have a copy and please, please don't throw those autographs away, OK?

When Jim signed his name "Arthur Rimbaud" for Nancy and Sheila, he was linking himself to more than 3000 years of poetic tradition. In that playful gesture he revealed as much about himself as in a dozen interviews.

Rimbaud was a favorite of Jim's, as much for his poetic theories as for his poems. In 1871, Rimbaud, a sixteen year old boy-poet wrote in a letter to a fellow French poet:

> The Poet makes himself a seer
> by a long, vast and reasoned
> derangement of all the senses—
> every form of love, of suffering,
> of madness.

Arthur, a long haired, unkempt, young idler did not, himself, originate this concept. He was merely re-echoing what he had read in the *ION*, where Plato quotes Socrates on the subject of poetic impulse:

> All great poets, epic as well as
> lyric, compose their beautiful
> poems not by art, but because
> they are inspired and possessed.
> Lyric poets are not in their right
> mind when composing their
> beautiful strains. For the Poet is a
> light and winged and holy thing,
> and there is no invention in him
> until he has been inspired and is
> out of his senses, and the mind is
> no longer in him. When he has not
> attained to this state, he is
> powerless and is unable to utter
> his oracles.

Jim said it this way:

> *Thank you, O Lord*
> *For the white blind light*
> *A city rises from the sea*
> *I had a splitting headache*
> *From which the future is made*

(JDM)

The tradition of the oracle, seer, prophet, poet, goes back much farther than 400 B.C. when Socrates taught. Primitive man's first chants were poetic prayers inspired by extreme sensory deprivations, natural hallucinogens or great emotional states. The poet-diviner comprehended and interpreted reality for his tribe, not by analysing trends or reading facts, but by evoking words, images, paradoxes and myths. As the power of the visions of the great religions waned, new visions conjured up by poetry and art were needed.

In the 1920's and '30's, the Surrealists called for new myths to fit the new technological man. Surrealism has to do with dreams and the irrational, with images that are unrestrained by reason or convention. Jim, in an interview, explained the Surrealist's manifesto: "Each generation wants new symbols, new people, new names. They want to divorce themselves from the preceding generation." In *An American Prayer* he wrote:

> *Let's reinvent the gods, all the myths*
> *of the ages*
> *celebrate symbols from deep elder forests*

(JDM)

Socrates reminded his pupils that poets had to be out of their minds to be truly divinely inspired. If they were, then their oracular revelations (*ie.* their words, poems and stories) could define man's place in the cosmos.

Rimbaud said that the poet is truly a stealer of fire. Through the vigorous and often unpleasant, if not painful, overthrow of the senses, poets could reach exceptional psychological states that fostered a deep communication with primal life forces.

In America, the tradition of evoking poetic oracles was followed by Edgar Allan Poe, a visionary poet, who achieved unusual psychic states through the use of opium, coffee, alcohol and lack of sleep. Walt Whitman, too, was a poet of the ecstatic. His "Song of Myself" seeks to reveal the oneness of all life while praising the freedom of each individual.

Out here in the perimeter
There are no stars
Out here we is stoned
Immaculate

(JDM)

In the years 1966 and 1967, Jim used LSD to journey to the frontiers of divine madness, seeking inspiration beyond the perimeter of reason. He was out there with Homer, Blake, Rimbaud, Poe, Whitman and others. The visions and portents he experienced were the breath and fire of his poems, lyrics and observations. Some of his visions were brilliant and clear, filled with universal mythological and symbolic images. Other times, what he saw was horrible and the words he put on paper could not adequately convey the abstract terror and nightmare transparency.

I think there's a whole region of
images and feelings inside us that
rarely are given outlet in daily life.
And when they do come out, they can take
perverse forms. It's the dark side.
Everyone, when he sees it, recognizes the
same thing in himself. It's a recognition
of forces that rarely see the light of day.
The more civilized we get on the surface,
the more the other forces make their plea.

(JDM)

Finally, Jim had exhausted the augury power of psychedelics. The human mind is infinite, but our capacity to experience infinity is finite. He stopped using LSD. He could take the trip without the drug; all he had to do was touch pen to paper.

Jim drank alcohol, in all its varieties, to excess. He knew he did. He drank, not for inspiration, but to quiet the ceaseless clamor of the demons, ghosts and spirits begging for release. Alcohol put his visions temporarily to rest and allowed him to relax and play. I doubt that he ever wrote one good line when he was drunk. He wrote, instead, in the clear, bright light of dawn, when the world was still and full of hope. In these quiet, intense hours, he spilled his poems out on the pages of dozens of notebooks. To this day, only a small fraction of his writings have been published.

Come, for all the world lies hushed
and fallen
Green ships dangle on the surface of ocean
And skybirds glide smugly along the planes
Gaunt crippled houses strangle the cliffs
In the cities a hum of life starting,
Now come

(JDM)

Almost all of his friends, and most of the journalists who chronicled his actions, saw Jim's lifestyle as self–destructive. But looking at it in the light of the ancient oracle/poet tradition, his lifestyle could be called self–instructive: a way of learning about the nature of things by risking the derangement of the senses. It was his occupation and vocation. He did it the way he did everything, without reservation and to the extreme limit of his abilities.

Meanwhile, his friends and contemporaries and the rock writers, gossip columnists and media mouths, viewed his excessive behavior as . . . excessive. I don't know of a single person who understood Jim's visionary lineage. A few of the writers were moved by his genius and appreciated his courage, but the rest called him crazy, pretentious, ridiculous, political, absurd, theatrical, erotic, sensual, stupid, obvious and revolting. They took his justly famous remark:

I am interested in anything about
revolt, disorder, chaos, especially
activity that seems to have no meaning.
It seems to me to be the road to freedom.

to mean he was an anarchist, a revolutionary, or worse, a nihilist. Hardly anyone noticed that Jim was restating Rimbaud and the Surreal poets, artists and thinkers like André Breton, Marcel Duchamp, Luis Bunuel and Louis Aragon.

Words dissemble
Words be quick
Words resemble walking sticks
Plant them, they will grow
Watch them waver so.

> *I'll always be a word man*
> *Better than a bird man*

(JDM)

He was a poet and had printed (at his own expense) a poem about the death of the Rolling Stones' guitarist, Brian Jones, "Ode to L.A. While Thinking of Brian Jones, Deceased." He distributed copies of this work to people who came to a Doors concert in Los Angeles. He also self published two books of poetry, *An American Prayer* and *The New Creatures*, as well as a series of observations and insights called *The Lords: Notes on Vision*. He gave copies of these books away to fans, friends and journalists.

On December 8, 1970, to celebrate his twenty-seventh birthday, he hired a recording studio to put several hours of his verse on tape. He invited a few of his friends to this unique birthday party: John Haeny, the recording engineer; Florentine Pabst; Kathy Lisciandro and me. I brought my camera.

Jim began that night's taping with a casual remark to John Haeny: "OK, let's do a bit and listen to it." The first poem he read hooked me:

In that year we had a great visitation
> *of energy*
Back in those days everything was simpler
> *and more confused*
One summer night, going to the pier I ran into
> *two young girls.*
The blonde was called Freedom.
> *The dark one, Enterprise.*
We talked and they told me this story.

(JDM)

He proceeded to read from the pages Kathy had typed for him for close to twenty minutes. Finally, John had to cut in and stop him because the tape had run out.

I couldn't absorb the onslaught of wild images and evocative words. These were new poems that I had not heard or read. I felt like a swimmer in heavy surf, OK as long as I let the waves of words carry me. When I tried to fight for meaning, or understanding, I was quickly underwater.

I walk through the panther's living room
And our summer together ended too soon
Stronger than farther
Strangled by night
Rested by sun burst
Relax in her secret wilderness
This is the sea of doubt which threads harps
Unwithered and unstrung
It's the brother not the past
Who turns sunlight into glass
It's the valley, it's me.
Testimony from a strange witness.

(JDM)

He was using words; not for their logic, but for their emotive effect. His words didn't have to mean so much as imply and suggest. He was more interested in getting a reaction from the whole body, rather than just the mind. He used words to construct a great mural of feeling. I closed my eyes and let him do it to me.

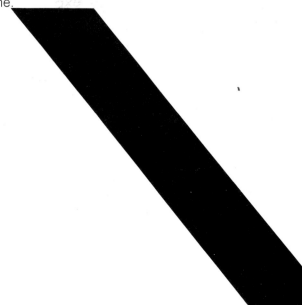

Jim and Florentine at the Lucky-U.

Finally, after another roll of tape wound to an end, Jim announced, "OK? Let's go get a taco." So we walked the two blocks to the Lucky-U, a Mexican bar and restaurant favored by UCLA film school students, both for it's fine, flavorful food, and its clientele of characters.

We each had a Mexican plate washed down by a couple of beers, and no one said a single word about poetry. What could we say? We were all still trying to grasp what we had experienced. Jim was in a great mood, fiesty, playful and happy to be recording his poems.

Back at the recording studio, Jim's birthday present from John Haeny, a bottle of Irish whiskey, shared by all of us, was almost gone. Jim was feeling frisky, but the alcohol and the vocal fatigue from almost two hours of constant reading were causing diction errors. He tripped and slurred his way past too many words.

He had decided to use a tambourine to accent lines or words. This became a problem when he insisted on shaking it right into the microphone before John could adjust the recording level.

Despite the occasional slurred words and the tambourine, Jim read an additional twenty pages before he decided it was time to have a little fun and try something new.

"All right, tell you what. Me and old Frank are gonna do what you call the old 'improvo-suto,' you know?"

This was the first I'd heard about it. John Haeny replied from the control booth, "Outta sight. You're free to move around out there. You don't have to hang around the mike if you don't want to."

Jim: "You ready?"
John: "Ready."

Jim smacked the tambourine against the mike and John learned he was not as ready as he thought. The tambourine smash, intensified by the headphones he was wearing, propelled John 1.6 feet up off the carpet. Before John could complain, Jim started to improvise a blues song.

At first the words consisted of stock blues-type phrases. I hoped Jim wasn't going to ask me to sing. I didn't want to deny him a birthday request, but on the other hand, I didn't fancy making a fool of myself on a tape that would probably outlive me.

After a few more verses and several tambourine shakes, Jim worked his way into a singing-talking delivery:

Come here, Frank,
Come here boy, I wanna talk to you.
C'mon!
Hey, look out folks,
I'm gonna bring my friend up here
          and we're gonna talk to you.
C'mon!
Well I say,
Frank
Are you cool?
And Frank says, yeah I am . . . cool.

He waited and I finally figured out I was supposed to say, "Cool," which I did.
Jim continued:

Well, you heard him say it.
Frank.
You hear him say it,
This man is what you wanna call. . . ."

I jumped in quick this time with my single syllable, "Cool."
Jim now broke back into his singing voice:

Cool, all right, let's go
Well, yeah, yeah, yeah
You know the man is cool
Wooa, yeah, yeah, yeah
You know the man is cool
Well, you know. . . .
This man. . . . He's
Cool. Wow.

And that was it. I was hoping he'd call it "Cool Frank " but I was relieved it was over.

Now Jim asked Kathy and Florentine to join him. Neither of them displayed any of my natural reserve. They were down from the control booth and into the studio in a flash.

Jim asked them to read in unison the woman's voice of a long narrative poem, while he would read the male voice. It usually takes a great deal of practice to fit two voices in unison, but Kathy's New York English and Florentine's German accent blended nicely in the one and only trial run Jim allowed them.

When the tape rolled, they got nervous and forgot to come in on cue and then started laughing and giggling for two minutes. Jim waited patiently.

After they had quieted down, he started his part again and this time they came in together at the right instant and read together beautifully, until they came to the line: "All of us have found a safe niche." Kathy pronounced the word "nich," the accepted American pronunciation, but Florentine, seeing a word that looked German, pronounced it "nickt." The girls heard each other's versions, stopped reading and broke into gales of laughter. They broke Jim up, too.

Jim: "Stop. Stop. Stop."
Florentine: "Well, do we say it the European way or the American way?"
Jim: "Nich, not nickt."
Florentine: "OK, I'm sorry."

Jim reads a poem as Kathy and Florentine await their cue.

Jim: "Ready?"
John: "Ready."
Jim: "OK, are you ready?"
Kathy: "OK, let's start."

They started up again, glancing at each other, but could not control their laughter when they came to the word "niche." Jim exclaimed, "Jeezo, wheezo," and laughed along with them.

It was very off-the-wall, but Jim was determined to continue. After a few practice runs at the line, the reading resumed. We all held our breath as the line approached: "All of us have found a safe niche. . . ." They got past it and sailed on to the next line: "Where we can store up riches." Kathy and Florentine continued to recite the next twenty-five lines in angelic unison, though slightly strange sounding English. Suddenly a loud CRASH made us all jump out of our socks. It was Jim, who listening with eyes closed, had started to doze, lullabied by the ladies' melodious voices. He lost his balance and pitched into the mike stands, which ended up on the hardwood floor with him.

He laughed as hard as we did and yelled, "Wait a minute! Wait a minute! Start 'em again. They're great."

John wanted to pack it in. It was late, his ears rang and he was the only one really working. "I think we got enough," he said.

Florentine would not hear of it. "What do you mean, John? We were right in the middle and you say we got enough. I want to do the whole thing all over again."

Jim and Kathy agreed with her. John good-naturedly replaced the mike. "All right. One more try," he told them, trying hard not to make it sound too much like a threat.

It went on for another hour: laughs, interruptions, mispronunciations, false starts and poems. At the end, Jim was moved to genuine, though booze amplified, admiration, "Brilliant, brilliant. Oh, my God, I couldn't believe it. This was incredible."

The ladies preened and bowed and smiled and tried to look humble, but Jim's praise delighted them. They were ready to continue reading all night.

The poetry Jim read on the night of December 8, 1970, and the poems he had recorded six months earlier, were to provide the bulk of the material for the poetry album he wanted to make, but never finished. Six years after his death, the remaining Doors, together with John Haeny, Corky Courson and I, spent long months working with Jim's poems. In November of 1978 Elektra Records released *An American Prayer*, the album of poetry Jim longed to make and which his friends had the privilege of completing for him.

We used to joke, as we toiled and argued in the recording studio, trying to fit Jim's words on vinyl, that the lead singer never showed up for any of the sessions. But almost everyday, in some way, he made his presence felt.

A HELL OF A WAY TO PEDDLE POEMS

BY ROBERT GOVER

I'd never heard of Jim Morrison and The Doors when, in 1967, I got a call from the editor of *The New York Times Magazine* suggesting I do a feature about them. Their first album, released quietly, was rising rapidly in the charts and having an astounding impact. After listening to it closely from start to finish, I was sure The Doors and their lead singer were something special in the contemporary music scene—and not only because of their sudden, stunning success. There was that certain unnameable something about their words and music that was strong, original and just right for the times. I was eager to get on with the job.

A luncheon was arranged and I anticipated talking to the group, learning how they'd developed such a distinct sound and how they were coping with the trauma of success. But the only member of the group who showed was Jim Morrison, and he let The Doors' management team do all the talking. Their managers, at that time, were wheeler-dealers, sharpies, and what they had to say was predictable, shallow and dull. Morrison seemed in a glowering mood, although now and then he caught my eye and made it clear by his intense stare that he had something to say. So after lunch we wandered off by ourselves and strolled through a park. That's when I met the widely read, philosophical, poetic Jim Morrison. We had an instant rapport, a *deja vu* effect, like we'd known each other in past lives. In the months that followed we saw a lot of each other.

Jim told me I could discount practically everything the management people had said because The Doors were planning to sever ties with them. Then he said that for him rock stardom was merely a step toward film making and that film making was an outlet for his poetry. "See, I'm really a poet."

What did he mean by poet? Did he mean he was a lyricist? "Yeah, that too, but basically I'm a *poet*." Whereupon he pulled out a notebook and read me a few of his most recently written pieces. They were brief, compact, philosophical and there was something about each poem that made me want to hear it again.

Our conversation then swung to the ancient tradition of poetry, written and spoken and sung, and I was amazed to find I was in the company of a young man who had studied the subject deeply. Indeed, there was no denying it—poetry was his passion. Soon we found ourselves jabbering away like we'd just picked up a conversation from yesterday and would continue it tomorrow, maybe for the rest of our lives.

We were to see a lot of each other in the coming weeks and months even though the *Times* retired me from the assignment. That happened when the editor called me to find out how I was doing and to tell me the perspective he expected was: Jim as "the creation and product of Machiavellian Hollywood puppeteers." I laughed and told him that was a ludicrous notion; Morrison was a poet with great promise and definitely his own man. The editor seemed to think I'd been so taken by Morrison's charisma (manufactured by his management) that I had lost my rightful senses. And so I allowed as the *Times*'d best get someone else to write the version he was looking for.

I was living at the time with a lady named Beverly Mitchell in a two-story apartment on the beach in Malibu. It had eight doors and we usually left them all unlocked. Jim liked to put in suprise appearances. We'd come home to find him sitting at my desk, picking over whatever I'd been writing. Or, we'd wake up around 4 a.m. hearing a prowler: Jim raiding the refrigerator. Or, I'd be upstairs at my typewriter and feel eyes on my back, turn and find him peeking over the decking of the upper balcony—having chinned himself to this position, hanging dangerously by white-knuckled hands, waiting for us to do something because it was a three-story fall to the beach below.

This last became his favorite entrance for it never failed to unsettle us. Bev would push up on his boots while I pulled on his arms and, after considerable drama, heightened by his noncooperation, we'd land the rising rock star on our upper balcony.

Naturally, whatever we'd have planned for the day would be arrested by such a show-stopper, so we'd usually light up a joint, go for a walk on the beach and cavort. Sometimes Jim had something particular he wanted to discuss; sometimes he just wanted to quietly relax. Around sundown Bev would cook up a dinner and, likely as not, just as we were about to sit down and eat Jim would say, "Ah I

136

left a girl . . . sitting in the car." So we'd bring in his latest pick-up and dine, talk, smoke, drink wine and play sides.

Occasionally our discussions were as neatly structured as doctoral dissertations. Usually, though, we both got crazed. We bounced from moments of exquisite spiritual togetherness to moments when we were ready to kill each other—or so it seemed. We were both intense and driven, rather than practical and ambitious, and recognized each other as fellow tourists in the land of Dr. Jekyll and Mr. Hyde. I was deep into my own study of the occult forces and Jim liked to sift through my collection of books on the subject, selecting paragraphs at random to read aloud, setting off another round of talk. On this subject, we usually chose our words carefully and used them sparingly for we were both well aware that words, thoughts made meaningful through sound, conjure and invoke the invisibles.

We talked about such earth-bound things as how to deal with commercial fame and fortune. My brief and lesser literary fame was nothing compared to the pressure cooker his rock star fame was fast becoming. It soon became clear that the Jim Morrison being created as a public image was a lot different from the Jim Morrison I was getting to know. Given his temperament it didn't take a fortune teller to foresee that this could lead to mind-blasting trouble.

One of our favorite topics was who really "owns" an art product. The person or persons who conjured it up? The ones who "packaged" it and got it out to the public? Or those who responded, absorbed it into their beings, "ate" it as a delicious aesthetic delicacy? Or was it forever the property of those famous invisibles called Muses? Although we could carry on such discussions with a minimum of words and a maximum of telepathy I had to be on guard, always, for the only thing one could expect from Jim was the unexpected.

One night, for instance, he punctuated our discussion by suddenly rushing to the turntable, yanking off The Doors' freshly released second album, smashing it to the floor and stomping it with his high-heeled boots, cursing it wildly. I rushed to him and angrily insisted he should destroy *his* copy of that album, not *mine*. That put us into a philosophical nuthouse for hours, which we both thoroughly enjoyed, since it forced us to think well beyond the usual ruts of rationality.

I must add that he later brought me another copy of that album. He even offered to autograph it but I got snitty and told him to just put it on and let's listen to it all the way through, without another ruckus.

Another aspect of our relationship was that Jim liked to drive my Olds 98 and I found it fun to be chauffeured about by a skyrocketing rock star. He drove a bit recklessly, but what the hell, he always got us there without a dent. I'd bought that monstrous vehicle in Las Vegas, where I'd lived for about a year, and I liked to spin yarns about that unique city, and Jim got a kick out of hearing about it. So it came about that we decided to take a trip there. His lady, aside from teenaged occasionals, was Pamela, so we planned to go as a foursome. But when the time came to depart, Jim and Pam got into a fight. We went instead as a threesome.

It's probably a good thing Pamela didn't come along, in light of the misadventure which befell us. Or maybe I should say that if she had come to Vegas, we'd never have gotten into the mess we got into. I don't know . . . the two of them together could be notorious emotional arsonists, or deft firefighters, depending on their mood at the time.

Some Vegas friends of mine gave us the red-carpet treatment when we arrived around sundown. One of them, Mike, was a Doors fan. The other, Chaney, had never heard of The Doors. As a party of three couples and Jim—dressed as usual in his tight leather pants—we had a jovial dinner, then decided to go out on the town. Chaney read off a list of shows playing and we all locked in on *Stark Naked and the Car Thieves*, playing at the Pussycat A Go Go.

Jim had been driving since noon, in a dour mood because of his tiff with Pamela, but the dinner and a glass of wine or two had lifted his spirits. We arrived at the Pussycat's parking lot in three cars, and Jim—ever alert to a dramatic entrance possibility—borrowed a Pall Mall from me and continued his method-acting studies by pretending it was a joint. He got out of the car and went with Mike and his lady toward the Pussycat's entrance, followed by Chaney and his lady, followed by Bev and me.

What happened next I can only attribute to the fact that we were a racially mixed group with two "hippies" and it was this mix that drove a Pussycat security guard bonkers. Affable Mike was leading the way, so he was first to encounter the pride and prejudice of the guard, who suddenly bashed him on the head with his billy club. From the parking lot, I saw Mike go down and heard him yell something like, "Hey, what the hell is this?" Then the guard came at Jim, who leaned against a wall and continued to placidly act out his joint smoking. The guard smacked Jim's head . . . again and again and again. Jim acted as though the guard wasn't there, even when blood began streaming down. Chaney rushed into this scene yelling, "This is an outrage, call the police!" Why the guard never hit Chaney, who is black, I'll never know—unless it's because Chaney is an ex-football star and looks it. Anyhow, Bev and I came jogging into this mess and the guard swung at me. I ducked and backed away and suggested in a loud voice that we go see some other show.

By this time the Pussycat's entrance was in a huge uproar, with more security guards arriving, people screaming, Mike in an Irish fury, Jim placidly bleeding, the ladies nearly hysterical, Chaney yelling, "Call the police" and me yelling, "Let's get out of here." The reason I was in favor of retreat was that I knew from experience Jim attracted cops like honey attracts bears. His charisma was such that your ordinary upholder of the established order could be infuriated merely by the sight of Morrison strolling down the street—innocent to all outward appearances but . . . well, there was that invisible something about him that silently suggested revolution, disorder, chaos.

That night the Vegas cops had been idling not far away and arrived pronto. It didn't surprise me when they took one look at this noise, grabbed Morrison and bent him over the hood of their patrol car. It did, however, cause me considerable fright when they grabbed me as the other "criminal" involved, because I had a real marijuana joint in my pocket, and that could get you a long stay in a Nevada prison.

But our guardian angels were on the job. Chaney's loud indignation distracted the policemen long enough for me to slip away to the shadows, drop the joint and resume the position of the friskee a wink before the cops were ready to search me.

After the frisk, the cops cuffed our hands behind our backs, just Jim and me, and shoved us into the patrol car and dutifully drove us toward the bars of justice. I was shaken due to the close call with the joint, Jim's head was still bleeding and, worse, his demons were bubbling up. Soon they were rushing out of his mouth like a pack of mad dogs attacking helpless strangers in the forest. "You chickenshit pigs, you redneck stupid bastards," etcetera and so forth. I made an effort to stem this tide of demons telling him to hush up and cool it, and Jim did try, but it was hopeless, for the demons had him now and were coming through in a hurricane of invectives.

It wasn't just our momentary plight that had roused these invisible avenging angel/demons—it was also the temper of the times, the war in Vietnam, the plight of millions all over the planet who are unjustly harmed by such uniformed nitwits as these. Morrison thought and felt in planetary terms, and his mind had an uncanny way of reaching way back in time, as though he were the reincarnation of a pagan priest who'd been burned at the stake during the Inquisition and was here to avenge that wrong, along with others. When manhandled by the emperor's troops, it seemed, he would rather be killed than humbled. In the heart and soul of Jim Morrison there was an uncontrollable rage against injustice. While it's true that he put people through psychological changes like you wouldn't believe, I never knew him to harm anyone physically—except himself. And then it was only to make a point, a statement he deemed important enough to suffer for.

At the police station we were roughly escorted to a large office space full of people at desks, tapping typewriters, reading reports, sipping coffee and performing other such police duties. Our "hippie-length" hair was not yet the fashion in Vegas, and our arresting officers had had more than they could take of Jim's "disrespect for the law." So they made us strip naked in front of all those officers, men and women, with the clear intention of humiliating us. "Let's see if they're boys or girls, har har har."

But Jim at age twenty-four was Mr. Body Beautiful and I'd been pumping iron and running, so neither of us felt much humiliation. Until, that is, they brought forth a spray gun and engulfed us in big clouds of roach powder, then made us turn around, bend over, spread our cheeks and gave us each a final blast in the ass. That brought laughter from the assembled peace officers, but was by no means the medicine needed to quiet Jim's obsessing demons.

By the time we'd been booked, fingerprinted, photographed and thrown into the holding tank, James Douglas Morrison was no longer present. His eyes were out of focus and he was panting like a fire-breathing dragon. That's when he climbed the bars of our extra-high cell and drew my attention to the assembled minions of law and order by yelling, "Hey, Bob, ain't they the ugliest motherfuckers you ever saw?" and other such endearments, delivered in that resonant voice and clear diction which was fast becoming his trademark as a singer. There was no point trying to remind him that the police have the extra-legal power to kill you, or worse, to beat you into a brain-damaged basketcase. Whatever force had gained control of him cared not one bit for the safety of his physical being or mine.

Presently our arresting officers returned to tell us they got off duty at midnight and that we would then "have a date, somewhere real private." Which only caused the ranting and raving coming out of Jim's mouth to become more eloquent and precisely phrased. Even from behind those bars he was determined to make a dream-haunting entrance into the consciousness of all within hearing.

I laid down on one of the steel bunks and concentrated on Bev and the others putting their wits together and getting us out of there before midnight. While Jim preached from his perch up the bars, I watched the secondhand sweep around the dial, the minutes go by . . . and soon enough we had only five to go.

Yes, they got us out, just in the nick of time, over Jim's protests that he wanted to call his lawyer in L.A. and file charges for false arrest. We'd been charged with public drunkenness, but walked out of that jail as sober as we'd gone in. We did, however, continue partying, and that got crazier and crazier.

Jim was—or seemed to be—calmer than the rest of us by the time we got back to the Pussycat parking lot to retrieve my car. He got behind the wheel and we all piled in, intending to repair to the Moulin Rouge for a quiet, soothing interlude of jazz. Then, just as we were beginning to relax and unwind, Jim decided to drive on the wrong side of the street, yelling about how he was now on a search-and-destroy mission for police cars.

At the first stoplight, Chaney grabbed him from behind and I ran around and got behind the wheel, and we continued on our way with Jim laughing like a maniac.

Before we'd finished our first round of drinks at the Moulin Rouge, Jim pulled another one out of his bottomless bag of show-stoppers. He was enchanted by this jazz combo and decided to join in, went up to the stage, picked up the mike and, for a warmup, let out one of his famous "Back Door Man" screams. The combo stopped playing, dumbfounded. None of them knew this strange behavior was being performed by a nationally famous rock-star; they thought he was a fullmoon lunatic and decided now was a good time to take a break.

Chaney, who'd had more than he could handle, grabbed Jim, hauled him outside and, by the time I got there, was threatening bodily harm if Jim didn't settle down and quit acting crazy. Jim loved every minute of this scolding, which only made Chaney angrier. Mike saved our partying by suggesting we all go to his apartment and listen to his Doors albums. Chaney said he didn't want to hear no damn Doors albums, but came along anyway and listened, utterly unimpressed. Bev and I soon retired to a bedroom, leaving the other ladies snoozing, as Mike and Chaney debated—and Morrison silently listened—the cultural worth, or lack thereof, of The Doors' music.

The next afternoon we went to a seafood place for raw oysters, then said our goodbyes. After the drive back to L.A., Jim took Bev and I to dinner, and then to the Whiskey on Sunset Strip, where Dr. Jekyll Morrison delivered an in-depth analysis of how The Doors had developed their music there, refining it in response to this more intimate and discerning audience. Since they'd become "bigtime," they were expected to play concerts for thousands of screaming teenagers, and this was already beginning to bore Jim.

Now, fourteen years later, there lingers a public impression of Morrison as being usually drunk, often brazenly lewd, and unable to hold up under the pressures of stardom. Gossip-mongering journalists dined upon that aspect of his personality like microbes feasting on a corpse. True, he did little to discourage that legend, and few of the journalists of the time made any effort to reveal that other, far more important aspect of him: his mind. It was, after all, his mind which has had such a powerful effect on millions of people. Being the mind of a poet, it was inclined to intoxications of great variety, intensity and subtlety.

And hidden behind the public legend, the private Jim Morrison diligently pursued his primary task: poetry. For all his famous outlandish pranks, he wrote an amazing amount of poetry, the quality of which continues to gain the attention of serious connoisseurs. Thus, in retrospect, it becomes clear that in his showmanship he reached back to the very roots of poetry to become, via the music of his time, a shaman.

I often thought his behavior was an attempt to "break on through" to an extrasensory view—a vantage point from which he could monitor the invisible causes of the events that swirled around his physical being. Certainly he was a student of the invisible powers that move people by affecting their thoughts and emotions. And, at the height of his singing career, he demonstrated an awesome ability to rouse crowds to screaming frenzy, then silence them, then rouse them to frenzy again. He could do more with a crowd of people than the U.S. government and Frank Sinatra combined.

Even now, a decade after his death, his recorded voice, his written and spoken words, have the power to jar people loose from enslaving assumptions.

One should remember that The Doors arose to prominence and had their initial impact at a crucial juncture in our nation's history. During the summer of 1966 when The Doors were developing their music on Sunset Strip, LSD was the object of Senate Hearings which led to its prohibition, the U.S. military bombed Hanoi for the first time, riots were erupting in the black ghettos of northern cities, Robert Speck killed eight nurses in their Chicago dormitory and Charles Whitman, ex-Marine and Boy Scout leader—shooting from the top of the clocktower at the University of Texas— hit forty-four people, killing fourteen.

The Doors' first album appeared in January of 1967, as the Pentagon announced that 5,008 American troops had died in Vietnam in 1966. The National Students Association admitted receiving $3 million from the CIA to spy on their fellow students. An anti-war demonstration in New York City drew 400,000 marchers. Heavyweight boxing champion Muhammad Ali was arrested for refusing army induction.

During the summer of '67 while "Light My Fire" held its grip on AM stations, riots broke out in the ghettos of 127 U.S. cities. Between July 12 and 17, 26 were killed in Newark, 1,500 were injured and 1,390 were arrested. From July 23 to 30 in Detroit, 43 died, 2,000 were injured, 5,000 arrested; 1,700 stores were looted, 1,445 buildings burned and 5,000 emerged homeless.

While this War between inner city blacks and the established order's gunmen was happening, tens of thousands of young people converged on San Francisco's Haight-Ashbury district for the famous "Summer of Love," outraging upholders of law and order with LSD, communal living, free love, marijuana, Eastern religions, spiritualism, "Acid Rock" and public burnings of draft cards.

Even with nuclear annihilation never far from awareness, there was an explosion of rage on both sides of the color line, much of it directed at the state's presumed right to confiscate young men's lives for a war that was meaningless to them. The Love Power of the Sixties had met the Protectors of the Status Quo and discovered a lot of them would rather kill than reason or debate. As the music of The Doors permeated the airwaves, groping the national psyche, black students died at Jackson State and Black Panthers across the country were raided and shot by the dozens. The Jim Morrison I knew realized he might soon become number one on the establishment's hit list.

Then in 1969 and '70, came the deaths of such rock stars as Brian Jones, Jimi Hendrix and Janis Joplin—who all died with fatal synchronization at age twenty-seven. Jim had commemorated Jones' passing with a poem titled "Ode To L.A. While Thinking of Brian Jones, Deceased," which he'd published at his own expense, and distributed to the audience at a Doors concert.

I knew nothing about that poem back then, for Jim and I went separate ways late in 1968. When I was handed a copy by Frank Lisciandro during the summer solstice of 1981, I was astounded . . . by the elegant words Jim used to empathize with Brian Jones' drowning; by the means he chose (consciously or intuitively) to predict his own death two years later; and by the sheer magical grace of the piece.

The last time I saw Jim was when he drove out to Malibu to tell me The Doors were going on a European tour, and ask if I'd come along and write a book about it. There was an impish glint in his eye as he contemplated delivering his lyrics over the language barrier. I was intrigued. Here was a chance for me, the storyteller, to be "ringside" when this David took on the Goliath of our Mother Culture. But I was having personal problems, and word was trickling in that my career was being sabotaged by reactionary elements. I told Jim about this, and said I'd have to decline.

Now, for the umpteenth time, I regret that decision, but what the hell . . . I might not have survived that trip to tell about it, for travelling with Morrison was like riding a rickety rollercoaster. Being a kamikaze pilot in the wild blue yonders of irrational consciousness, Jim lived that old Native American saying, "Hey! Today is a good day to die!"

When the official announcement of his death came in 1971, I was skeptical. Had any companies held business risk insurance policies on Morrison and those other dead rockers? If so, who had collected, and how much? And why had it been those among the most politically influential who had died? Was it simply in step with the tradition of Western art for such luminous personalities to bow out at young ages?

Then there was the suspicion that Jim had rigged his supposed death with Pamela's help, shedding his rock star identity so he could get on with his real work, poetry. It wasn't the first time rumor had circulated that he'd departed this life. All we were left with was Pamela's word, a French death certificate and an unmarked French grave. Well, it was a fittingly mysterious exit for such a rare and gifted showman/shaman. Dead or alive, I'm sure Jim loves it that nobody knows for sure. The first day we met, what was uppermost in his mind was the book of poems he was then working on—how could he get it published and taken seriously without his rock 'n' roll image interfering? It wasn't until after 1971 that large numbers of people learned that rock star was his job and poetry was his real work.

Well, Jim it was a hell of a way to peddle poems but you pulled it off. Magnificent. There's no arguing with success. Congratulations, wherever you are.

Ode to LA while thinking of Brian Jones, Deceased

I'm a resident of a city
They've just picked me to play
the Prince of Denmark

Poor Ophelia

All those ghosts he never saw
Floating to doom
On an iron candle

Come back, brave warrior
Do the dive
On another channel

Hot buttered pool
Where's Marrakesh
Under the falls
the wild storm
where savages fell out
in late afternoon
monsters of rhythm

You've left your
Nothing
to compete w/
Silence

I hope you went out
Smiling
Like a child
Into the cool remnant
of a dream

The angel man
w/Serpents competing
for his palms
& fingers
Finally claimed
This benevolent
Soul

Ophelia

Leaves, sodden
in silk

Chlorine
dream

mad stifled
Witness

The diving board, the plunge
The pool

You were a fighter
a damask musky muse

You were the bleached
Sun
for TV afternoon

horned-toads
maverick of a yellow spot

Look now to where it's got
You

in meat heaven
w/the cannibals
& jews

The gardener
Found
The body, rampant, Floating

Lucky Stiff
What is this green pale stuff
You're made of

Poke holes in the goddess
Skin

Will he Stink
Carried heavenward
Thru the halls
of music

No chance.

Requiem for a heavy

That smile
That porky satyr's
leer
has leaped upward

into the loam

→ 10 A   → 11   → 11 A

"The media is the message and the message is me." (JDM)

→ 13 A   → 14   → 14 A

"Whoever controls the media controls the mind."(JDM)

In the early rounds Ted led with a fast combination of Poe, Artaud and Rimbaud. Jim counterpunched with Breton, Burroughs and Blake. Ted jabbed with T.S. Eliot and Hemingway. Jim shot out a quick right with Carl Jung. Ted feinted with Blaise Cendars; Jim jabbed with John Lennon, catching Ted with his guard down. He fought back weakly with Zappa, but Jim pinned him to the ropes with John Lee Hooker and Sam Cooke.

I went and got another round of Bohemias.

By the time I got back the tape was on side two and Ted was into incest, patricide, Oedipal yearnings and sex. Jim ignored all of it and suggested a game of pool.

Morrison was only a fair pool player and I am below average, but Ted was the worst pool player west of the Rockies. A blind-folded fish could have sunk him. Still, he seemed to have lots of fun and he kept putting quarters in the slot. After six games of ''8 ball'' and another two beers, the interview resumed.

Jim was warmed up and at his very best. Words and phrases sparkled from his mouth and tingled when they touched the tape. Ted vibrated with unrestrained delight. It was going to be a terrific interview. His editor would love it. Jim provided a thousand great quotes:

''The sensual remorse of early rock''; ''The violent angels of change''; ''Music inflames temperament''; ''All art is essentially intercepted energy''; ''The Doors as Avatars of chaos''; ''Money beats soul every time.''

The words rolled out of Jim faster than Ted could interject questions. Soon two 60-minute cassettes were filled and we'd all had enough.

We took Ted back to the Doors' office, where Jim gave him a copy of *The Lords*. Ted was so grateful that he momentarily lost his journalistic objectivity and confessed that he had always disliked the Doors music because it was ''. . . too dark and gloomy,'' but he really loved Jim's lyrics. ''Illuminating'' was the word he used. He left promising to send Jim a final draft of the article for approval and shaking his hand in eternal gratitude.

''Let's see what ol' Ted does with all that,'' Jim said. ''Wanna bet he makes me look like a yo-yo?''

''A leather clad yo-yo with a sexy top spin and cunning lyrics,'' I replied. Mexican beer makes me articulate.

''A yo-yo is a yo-yo is a yo-yo,'' Jim declared.

The article came out about three months later. The 4500 words were given a prominent feature space in the magazine. It was a publicist's dream of free ink. Naturally, it was a complete downer to read. Ted had turned a pleasant afternoon of beer, pool and talk into a drunken brawl in a dive on the wild side of Hollywood. He characterized me as Jim's ''drinking buddy.'' I thanked my sense of self-preservation that I never gave him my last name. The article tore Jim apart. Ted took quotes out of context and used answers for questions never posed. It was a slick job of verbal assassination. Sure, the facts were there, but the truth was missing.

Jim was non-plussed. He pointed out how his key phrases adorned the page in bold-faced type.

''You were right,'' I told him, ''he made you look like an amplified yo-yo.''

''At least he used most of the stuff I gave him.''

''You're not pissed off?'' I was boiling mad.

''I expected it.''

''But he cut you up.''

''So, what am I supposed to do? If I say no to interviews, they make up stuff or try to interview my dog or read my garbage. No thanks. I'd rather give 'em a shot at me and land a few good punches myself.''

''You're weird, man. I'd want to kill that East Coast jerk if I was you.''

''Ultimately, I come out ahead, right? He quotes me and the quotes look good. It makes Elektra happy, it makes the band happy and we sell more records.''

''He called you: 'The bozo prince of pretentious rock.' ''

''Sticks and stones will break my bones, but. . . .''

''OK, OK, you're right. But I'd still like to punch him out.''

Finally though, it was words that hurt Jim the most. Like the tragic characters in the classic Greek dramas he read and reread, Jim became a victim of hubris, the arrogance and pride in his own ability with words. He was blind to the great, slow–churning power of the press. He had an overwhelming conviction that he could deal with words better than anyone else. His belief that he could control the media was his fatal flaw.

He tried to manipulate the media by feeding it headlines, great big vivid canvases of words and phrases like *"The Doors are erotic politicians."* When Jim said "erotic politicians" he meant it to be ironic and symbolic, a way to get instant attention. It was a buzz-word, a banner to be used like a concert poster. Jim expected it to stay up for a little while and then be torn down and replaced by another poster—another buzz-word.

Instead, "erotic politicians," and all the other phrases, were processed and re-processed, analyzed and reviewed. They travelled from publication to publication, even ending up in his own record company's publicity. The press took Jim's next phrase and did the same to it and then the next and the next. Eventually, they had a whole arsenal of his own words ready to type, ink and print. If he got in trouble in Phoenix, out came all the buzz-words flowing along the wire services, meaning to categorize, explain, condemn, satirize or ridicule him.

Jim became a victim of his own great ability to put words together. With the aid of hindsight, it is easy to say he should have been more humble. Maybe, at first, he was humble, or as humble as his talents allowed. Maybe he was actually trying to help all those interviewers and reporters.

Before he left for Paris, a particularly upsetting article appeared in a music rag. The article claimed Jim had lost his great emotive voice and that his writing was blocked. The writer claimed that Jim was a has-been rock idol and a never-been poet and that the Doors were an "interesting" but minor sidebar to American rock 'n' roll history. Jim was disappointed and despondent.

"I gave that guy a good interview. I even gave him a copy of my book. I should ask for it back."

"You should become less available to these morons," I said.

"Well, in Paris I won't be able to speak the language so they'll have a hard time interviewing me."

"You should avoid anyone carrying a portable cassette recorder."

"I think this one has finally cured me. I'm going to kiss the press off."

"That's what you said about falling out of windows."

Babe Hill, Jim, and attorney Max Fink, after a day's fishing in the Bahamas, 1970.

Jim getting ready for an afternoon of touch football, Redondo Beach, California, 1971.

We scaled the wall
We tripped through the graveyard
Ancient shapes were all around us
No music but the wet grass
                felt fresh beside the fog
Two made love in a silent spot
One chased a rabbit into the dark
A girl got drunk and balled the dead
And I gave empty sermons to my head
Cemetary cool & quiet
Hate to leave your sacred lay
Dread the milky coming of the day
I'd love to stay
I'd love to stay
I'd love to stay

(JDM)